Sports Strength

OTHER BOOKS BY KEN SPRAGUE

The Athlete's Body
The Gold's Gym Book of Bodybuilding
The Gold's Gym Book of Strength Training
The Gold's Gym Weight Training Book
Weight and Strength Training for Kids and Teenagers

SPORTS STRENGTH

Strength Training Routines to Improve Power, Speed, and Flexibility for Virtually Every Sport

KEN SPRAGUE

PHOTOGRAPHY BY JOHN BAUGUESS

Illustrations by Kiki Metzler

A PERIGEE BOOK

The strength-training routines in this book are intended for healthy individuals. People with health problems should not follow these routines without a physician's approval. Before beginning any exercise or nutrition program, always consult with your doctor. Children should always be supervised by an adult while performing these exercises.

Perigee Books
are published by
The Putnam Publishing Group
200 Madison Avenue
New York, NY 10016

Library of Congress Cataloging-in-Publication Data

Sprague, Ken.
    Sports strength : strength training routines to improve power,
  speed, and flexibility for virtually every sport / Ken Sprague ;
  photography by John Bauguess.
        p.   cm.
    Includes bibliographical references.
    ISBN 0-399-51802-9
    1. Weight training.   2. Weight training—
  Physiological aspects.   3. Exercise.   I. Title.
  GV546.6.S69   1993   92-21472 CIP

Cover design by Andrew M. Newman
Cover photo © by John Bauguess

Printed in the United States of America
1   2   3   4   5   6   7   8   9   10

This book is printed on acid-free paper.

To my most valued training partners,
my wife and children, Donna, Ken Jr., Julie, and Chris,
for their companionship and inspiration

CONTENTS

ACKNOWLEDGMENTS

I am grateful to Jeremy Tarcher for his interest in and enthusiasm for this book as well as our other past collaborative projects. A respected leader in New Age publishing, Jeremy contributes to improvement of our physical, mental, and spiritual well-being.

It was my good fortune to have Daniel Malvin (at Jeremy P. Tarcher) and Laura Shepherd (at Perigee Books) as editors; their steady support and good editorial judgment were invaluable. As well, I extend my sincere gratitude to Marian Castinado for her carefulness, her insight, and her interest in the book as she read and edited each chapter.

For their resourcefulness as research assistants, I thank Donna Wong and John Lassen, who helped me gather information and track down references. I acknowledge the following authors, who have considerable experience in the training and testing of athletes and who have stimulated my thoughts with respect to this publication: David N. Camaione, Ph.D., FACSM; Joe Chandler, Ed.D., Lander College; Brian P. Conroy, M.A., CSCS; Jack L. Groppel, Ph.D.; Dr. Gary R. Hunter, University of Alabama at Birmingham; Patrick Jacobs, M.S. CSCS; Mark Johnson, U.S. Olympic wrestling team, and head wrestling coach, Oregon State University; Jim Klinzing, Ph.D., Cleveland State University; Jim Lathrop, M.S. Ed., CSCS; Lee J. Morrow, strength and conditioning coach, East Tennessee State University; David Ohton, strength and conditioning coach, San Diego State University; Dr. Patrick O'Shea, professor of exercise and sport science, Oregon State University; Bogdan C. Poprawski, Ph.D., University of Toronto; Lynne Stoessel, M.S., CSCS; William Stearn, CSCS; Leo M. Totten, M.S., U.S. Weightlifting Federation; and Dr. Charles Yesalis, professor of exercise and sport science, Pennsylvania State University.

A special thanks to the athlete-models in the exercise demonstrations: Bruce Budzik, Owen Engelmann, Heather Fitzgerald,

Nathan Funnell, Shyda Gilmer, Robert Hausmann, Emilio Hernandez, Jr., Andrew Hunt, John Lassen, Sandy Newton, Ember Parks, Larry Smith, Lori Sonneburg, Chris Sprague, Jennifer Waldrop, and Kendra Yamamoto. And thanks to our photographer, John Bauguess, and his assistant, Ron Finne, whose patience and expertise are deeply appreciated. For her imaginative artistic skills and optimism in illustrating the book, I thank Kiki Metzler. I am grateful to Southside Fitness Club and Carole Kabot for the use of the gym facility for the photo sessions.

Finally, I want to acknowledge Chris Sprague, whose interest in weight training and sports provided the motivation for this book.

PREFACE

A stronger athlete is a better athlete—and all major sports substantiate this axiom. The force and speed of every step, jump, punch, or throw depends on strength, and that's equally true in elementary school basketball, high school volleyball, and professional football.

Sports Strength is an aggregate of my experience as a teacher, competitive athlete, and coach, including thirty-five years of strength-training experience, with a decade as owner of the original Gold's Gym, the world-famous mecca of weight training. Along the way, I've strength-trained countless athletes, both beginners and world champions, and seen the same results: improved performance, no matter what the sport.

There are countless bodybuilding books available, but their emphasis is on merely improving physical appearance. *Sports Strength* is for athletes, people who are devoted to strengthening athletic movements. Only an individualized program for your body and your sport can accomplish that, and *Sports Strength* gives you the information you need to tailor a strength-training program to your sport's specific needs.

Part One explains the physiological connection between strength training and sports performance, including what children, adolescents, and adult strength trainers need to keep in mind. It examines a strength trainer's nutritional needs, and answers common questions about a controversial subject: steroids.

Part Two reviews numerous training principles and styles, and explains the guidelines of training, including sets, reps, and weights. It also includes a full chapter on avoiding and treating injury.

Part Three gives you the components to design your individual workout. It begins with the Sports Strength Program—a workout that strengthens the entire body through five basic movements.

Next are supplementary exercises, and specialized performance programs to improve jumps, leg speed, grip, swing, and overhand throws. Finally, detailed training programs for your particular sport—categorized by age, training season, and even the different positions of various team sports—allow you to push the limits of athletic performance and achieve the competitive edge over opponents who don't strength-train.

If you're ready to reach your potential, take the next step toward improved sports performance. Regardless of your age, sex, size, or present fitness level, you can become a stronger, better, faster athlete—all through strength training. Let's start!

Part One

HOW STRENGTH TRAINING WORKS

CHAPTER 1

STRENGTH TRAINING MAKES A BETTER ATHLETE

Jose Canseco swings his bat, and the ball explodes 450 feet over the center-field wall. The fans stomp and scream as he circles the bases. Canseco's a natural power hitter, right? Wrong.

Star athletes like Jennifer Capriati, Bo Jackson, and Michael Jordan weren't born with their incredible abilities. They made it to the pros after years of top-notch strength training that improves speed, power, flexibility, technique, and muscular endurance.

Strength training existed as far back as the sixth century B.C., when Olympic wrestler Milo of Crotona lifted his baby bull each morning. As the animal grew, Milo grew stronger. This strategy—now known as *progressive resistance training*—became the basis for all strength-training programs.

Milo's theory was unique in his time, but today all superior athletes use specialized training, and are measurably stronger, bigger, and faster than those of the previous generation.

Strength training has dramatically changed the male athlete's body. Three-hundred-pound linemen—once a professional novelty—are now seen on college teams. But strength training has had an even greater impact on females. Twenty-five years ago, women weren't found in weight rooms. Now women often outnumber men, and the gender gap in sports performance is rapidly narrowing. Females are swimming faster than male champions did at the 1968 Olympics, and jumping higher than any male jumped until the 1956 Games. These great gains in physical strength, size, and performance are directly attributable to correct strength training, which builds the fundamental physiological elements of sports performance and helps prevent injuries.

Regardless of your sport or level of competition, you can strength-train to improve your performance. My ten-year-old son was the National Junior Olympic Champion in the shot put after a year of strength training. Alessandro Andrei was the 1984 Olympic Champion in the shot after fifteen years of strength training. Countless athletes—from middle-school tennis players to professional boxers—use strength training to achieve outstanding sports performance.

Strength training changes your body according to some simple rules of biology. Let's explore those changes and how they can make you a better athlete.

IS ATHLETIC ABILITY GENETICALLY LIMITED?

Are genetics important factors in athletic success? The *Los Angeles Times* has reported that thirteen father/son pairs have played in the NBA: Ed and Danny Manning; Bob and Danny Ferry; Leroy and LeRon Ellis; Wayne and Rex Chapman; Dolph and Danny Schayes; Butch and Jan van Breda Kolff; George and Larry Mikan; Earle and Sean Higgins; Press and Pete Maravich; Al and Allie Maguire; Matt and Matty Guokas; Jim and John Paxson; and Ernie and Kiki Vandeweghe.

Different genes produce enormous variations in height, eye color, and physical proportions. The range of genetically determined abilities is probably just as broad. Fifty thousand genes combine to program your body's development, performance, and internal and external structure. As a result, your absolute physical performance and strength are limited.

Can the athlete override that genetic limit? It depends. Consider this: Growth hormone is necessary for normal height, but if a child's genes designate too little, injections can override the program. Modern chemistry supersedes the genetic limit.

Strength training progressively overloads muscles, producing physical changes that increase the muscles' strength. But the strength increase appears to be limited by the endocrine system's genetically determined ability to produce testosterone, a hormone integral to muscular development.

Some athletes have injected themselves with "anabolic steroids" that augment the body's natural testosterone supply. The hypodermic syringe becomes a strongly productive gland, overriding the athlete's genetic limits. For more on steroids, and the adverse consequences of tampering with genetic programs, read chapter 6.

Successful athletes learn to work with limitations. Rely on quickness rather than trying to "play tall" if you're shooting-guard size. Develop great strength to compensate for less speed if you're an offensive lineman. In short, use training and playing strategies to accommodate your natural abilities.

Next, we'll explore several ways in which the body adapts to strength-training stresses.

HOW DOES STRENGTH TRAINING CHANGE THE BODY?

A muscle becomes stronger or weaker in response to the demands placed on it. Train hard, and a muscle grows stronger; don't exercise, and it grows weaker. The body *adapts*.

Biology students learn that adaptation through natural selection has been the survival mechanism of life on earth for four billion years. Over countless generations, life-forms changed physically in response to environmental stress.

Sports-training programs seek to produce adaptation in the athlete's body; this book contains several strength-training programs, because everyone has different needs and capacities for change. Spend your energy making the physical changes that are most important to your personal athletic success.

WHAT ARE THE STAGES OF CHANGE?

Although each body adapts differently, all adapt to strength training in the same three-stage sequence, roughly following Hans Selye's *general adaptation syndrome*.

The first stage of adaptation syndrome is *shock*. The muscle is stunned by a weight it is unaccustomed to lifting, and the overload may initially produce sore muscles and a strength decrease.

The second stage, *adaptation*, is an interrelated web of physiological changes that increase the muscle's ability to handle the overload. The same weight no longer causes stress. No soreness follows the workout. Strength increases.

In the third stage, *staleness*, the muscle easily meets existing demands. No further strength gains will occur unless the muscle must lift an even heavier weight.

This general sequence applies to all strength gains. However, the precise mechanics, whether an increase in muscle size or an increase in nerve/muscle interaction, depends on your age, sex, and training experience.

HOW DOES INCREASED STRENGTH HELP ATHLETES?

The word "strength" describes the muscle's ability to produce force in a single effort. For the athlete, strength increases the force of every push, pull, heave, swing, thrust, or jump.

There's no question in the coaching or scientific community that strength training builds strength. All else being equal, stronger muscles make a better athlete. In gymnastic terms, a muscle's contraction strength is the force needed to push or pull a barbell. In the stadium, strength is the muscular contraction's force as the athlete pushes against the ground while running and jumping, or the force that moves the body of an opposing lineman.

Skeletal muscles, so called because each is attached to two bones, produce the force in sports. Without the skeletal muscles' contraction, the athlete would not move, because when a nerve impulse signals the skeletal muscle to contract (shorten), that force is what pulls the attached pair of bones.

The synchronized contractions of hundreds of skeletal muscles produce myriad athletic movements. Just imagine the interplay of contractions needed to propel a pole vaulter down the runway and over the bar.

The good news: You can improve any muscular contraction through strength training. In fact, it's the *only* way beyond normal growth and development.

HOW DOES THE MUSCLE CHANGE?

Strength training isn't magic. Muscle tissue makes real physical changes that account for the increased strength. Here's an abbreviated list of the transformations that happen in the muscle cell long before they are visible to the naked eye:

1. The muscle cell gets larger. Myofibrils, the machinery that makes contraction possible, increase in number and size.
2. On a molecular level, the muscle cell stores more energy deposits and enzymes required by short-duration, high-strength contractions.

HOW DOES THE NERVOUS SYSTEM CHANGE?

Changes occur outside the muscle cell, too. Through strength training, the athlete's nervous system learns to signal more muscle cells to assist a contraction. These newly working muscle cells were always present. They just weren't needed to accommodate the previous strength demands.

The expanded interactions between nerve and muscle are called *neural adaptations*. Neural adaptations are thought to account for the rapid progress during the first months of weight training, as well as children's amazing strength-rate increases from strength training.

As the name implies, neural adaptations involve a nerve. A *motor neuron* (a nerve connected to muscle cells), signals muscles cells to initiate a contraction. Each motor neuron connects to and signals different numbers of muscle cells, from tens to thousands. Collectively, a motor neuron and its complementing muscle cells is a *motor unit*. The average muscle has thousands of motor units. As the signal passes along the motor neuron, the motor unit's muscle cells all simultaneously contract.

A muscle's contraction strength depends on the number and size of the motor units called into action. Whether you are lifting a feather or a dumbbell, the central nervous system (brain and spinal cord) computes the force requirements and activates the number of motor units needed to complete a task.

Strength training theoretically teaches the body to use existing motor units more efficiently, as the active units' firing rate is increased. Also, more motor units are involved in the contraction, making it stronger. Possibly strength training overrides inhibitors that prevent maximum force production.

HOW FAST CAN STRENGTH INCREASE?

The answer depends on the athlete's physical condition and age when beginning to strength-train.

Researchers working with preadolescent athletes document strength increases of up to 50 percent after only twenty weeks of strength training. That equals lifting one hundred pounds for every sixty-seven pounds previously lifted. Preadolescents cannot improve at this rate indefinitely, but gains do continue.

Adult athletes who had never lifted before experience the same phenomenon. Credible studies have reported a doubling of strength after only a year of training. As with preadolescents, though, once adult athletes have strength-trained for a considerable time, the gains slow.

IS THERE A LIMIT TO STRENGTH GAINS?

Practically speaking, no. Each year of strength training will allow you to lift heavier weights. And increased strength is never wasted on an athlete: It results in hitting or throwing a ball farther, running faster, jumping higher, or tackling with more power.

Some sports demand more than others, but all share a common truth: Increased strength is a competitive advantage available only to strength-trained athletes.

HOW DOES STRENGTH TRAINING BUILD POWER?

Strength training builds power, and the so-called power events—most notably football and track and field's throws—were the first to accept strength training.

But what is power? A physicist defines it as work done, divided by the time taken. Work is done when a force moves an object, such as launching a rocket ship into space. It's calculated in terms of watts and joules—units elusive to many nonscientists.

The athlete can consider power a combination of strength and speed. Whether throwing, punching, or batting, power is calculated by multiplying the movement's strength (force) by the movement's speed: Power = Strength × Speed.

As a result, the athlete's power increases with greater strength or speed. Surprisingly, *strength training also improves speed*, thus increasing both power factors!

Added power improves the body's *explosive movements*: vertical jumps, punching, shot-putting, batting, the sprinter's foot driving against the ground, and a swimmer's repeated strokes— motions demanding great force performed with great speed.

For young or old athletes, male or female, greater strength builds greater power. And a more powerful athlete is always a better athlete.

HOW DOES STRENGTH TRAINING BUILD SPEED?

Sprinters improve speed by increasing stride length and frequency. Tennis players train to serve with more speed, and volleyball players work for greater speed on a smash. In all cases, the athlete's muscles control speed.

The connection is this: A stronger muscle overcomes resistance—whether an athlete's own body weight, a bat, a discus, or a bicycle gear—more easily.

Imagine a sprinter in a hundred-yard dash. Now imagine her twice as strong. Twice the strength calculated into the leg drive's force allows her to overcome gravity more easily, extending her stride's length and frequency.

Research has verified what coaches long suspected: speed is highly specific. An athlete may have fast arms but slow legs, for example. Whether vaulting, sprinting, spiking, or throwing, hundreds of muscles synchronize to perform thousands of coordinated contractions each second. Each muscle can be trained for increased speed, emphasizing strength training's positive role in producing stronger, faster athletes.

HOW DOES STRENGTH TRAINING IMPROVE FLEXIBILITY?

In the past athletes from bygone eras often thought that weight training would make them "muscle-bound," an antiquated term referring to inflexibility. But as more and more athletes succeeded through strength training, the fear of weights was wisely discarded. In fact, scientific evidence indicates that strength training actually *improves* a joint's functional range when exercises are performed through a full range of motion. A study comparing various athletes' flexibility found Olympic weight lifters to be second only to competitive gymnasts!

HOW DOES STRENGTH TRAINING BUILD ENDURANCE?

Strength training has little effect on cardiovascular endurance, but it has a large impact on muscular endurance—the repetitions a muscle can perform against a fixed resistance. It increases the number of times per minute that the biceps can curl a fifty-pound barbell, or a sprinter can churn his legs.

Muscular endurance is a quality quite different from strength—though there is a correlation between the two—and training for muscular endurance improves only the muscles being worked.

HOW DOES INCREASED ENDURANCE CHANGE A MUSCLE?

Here are the most significant physical changes that a muscle undergoes to increase endurance:

1. The muscle tissue's blood cells (myoglobin) increase. This increases blood supply to the muscle, allowing greater oxygen and nutrient delivery.
2. The number of mitochondria (energy factories) increase in the cell, to sustain the longer muscular exertion.
3. The muscle tissue can transport more oxygen from the bloodstream to the mitochondria, where it is needed during energy production.

Endurance training stimulates neural adaptations. The adaptation's exact nature is poorly understood; however, the nervous system always fatigues more rapidly than the muscle tissue.

Just remember that strength training produces adaptations, preparing the muscle to contract more efficiently during single or low-repetition athletic movements; muscular-endurance training produces adaptations that prepare the muscle for numerous low-strength contractions. The adaptations depend on the training program's design, and they produce different physiological results.

HOW DOES STRENGTH TRAINING IMPROVE TECHNIQUE?

Success in any sport, from football to fencing, requires a highly stylized sequence of technical skills—the sport's *technique*.

Too little strength often blocks the aspiring athlete from learning correct technique. Imagine teaching rope climbing's coordinated movements to a child who lacks the upper-body strength to perform a single pull-up.

Other times, athletes unknowingly compensate for inadequate strength with poor technique. Young athletes are particularly vulnerable, because their genetic program increases leg strength before shoulder girdle and arm strength. As a result, power generated by the legs and passing through the torso can dissipate at the shoulder girdle. Consequently, when young people participate in sports requiring power generation or transmission through the shoulder girdle, bad habits develop, timing is destroyed, or optimal power is never realized. Strength training, however, can quicken nature's developmental pace, increasing transmission through the shoulders.

The midsection is often another weak link, even among athletes with extensive strength-training experience. Many train incorrectly, executing high-repetition, endurance-building sets rather than low-rep, high-resistance sets. For example, they might do fifty sit-ups with no weight, rather than ten repetitions with a weight held behind the head. The training program's design determines its effect on the muscle, whether abdominals or biceps. A strength program builds strength; an endurance program builds endurance.

Shot-putting offers an excellent example of the connection between weak physical links and faulty technique. Often the athlete doesn't exert maximum leg drive because he fears injuring the midsection. In other instances, the midsection cannot transfer the leg drive's force to the shoulders and arms. In both cases, poor technique and performance result.

Weight training, by strengthening specific muscle groups as well as the whole body, provides a valuable tool for correcting technical flaws.

HOW DOES STRENGTH TRAINING INCREASE SIZE?

At the beginning of this chapter, I noted that strength training is primarily responsible for modern athletes' greater muscular size. Football players aren't the only athletes who are bigger than those of past decades. Sprinters, boxers, weight-throwers, and wrestlers are larger too. At first glance, it appears that muscle strength and size go hand in hand.

Must a muscle grow bigger to become stronger? Need a muscle become stronger in order to grow bigger? Do muscles get larger by increasing the number of cells or the size of existing cells? Can females grow big muscles? Can children increase strength without increasing muscle size? These questions are collateral to muscle growth.

A full answer to these questions depends on a complex analysis of the athlete's age and sex. Look for those answers as you read chapters 2 through 4.

HOW DOES STRENGTH TRAINING PREVENT INJURIES?

Sports medicine practitioners have long recognized strength training as a valuable healing aid. After a physical therapist removes an atrophied limb from a cast, the patient begins a strength-training program to restore size, strength, and flexibility.

More recently, weight training has become a tool for injury prevention. During the 1970s and 1980s, research documented a positive correlation between resistance training and fewer incidents of injury and pain to tennis players and swimmers. This led to weight training's general acceptance as an injury-prevention aid.

Strength is a safety net. Stronger muscles can better absorb acceleration's quick stops and starts, whether the force is a foot hitting the ground, or a competitor's body block. Strength also improves joint stability, whether at the knee, hip, ankle, or shoulder. Let's explore this connection further.

The rotator cuff, a group of four muscles, stabilizes the shoulder, keeping the head of the humerus against the shoulder-blade socket. Damage to these muscles usually results from a collision or hard throw, when the muscle tissue was not prepared to withstand the violent contractions. Rotator cuff injuries have destroyed numerous athletic careers.

A stronger muscle has a better chance of surviving contractions because it has a greater range of safe operation. In other words, what is an overload for one athlete's muscles might be well within the tolerance of an athlete with a stronger rotator cuff.

Strength training also strengthens bones. Bone adapts to training stress by adding mineral content, and the additional minerals increase the bone's cross-sectional area and density. The stronger, thicker, more densely packed bone can better absorb the stress of athletic activity. Even without the other benefits, this would be justification enough to include strength training in an overall regimen. You can find more on increased bone strength later in the book.

RESULTS: AN OVERVIEW

Strength training improves the athlete's strength, speed, power, flexibility, muscular endurance, and technique, and prevents injury. All are important factors in athletic competition.

Strength training stresses the body, pushing it past a comfortable level. In turn, the body adapts by physically changing to comfortably accommodate the same stress level in the future. These changes provide the physical foundation for improved athletic performance.

People usually think of muscles when considering strength training's benefits; strength and size do increase, but not in isolation from the body's other systems. Endocrine glands secrete hormones needed to synthesize protein for muscle-tissue growth and maintenance. The cardiovascular system delivers more blood to the exercised tissue, providing needed hormones and nutrients, and the nervous system adapts by orchestrating more muscle cells into a contraction.

An individual's maturational level limits the nervous system's adaptational range, however. Maximum strength, maximum muscle growth, and refined skills cannot be achieved until neural maturity, which coincides with sexual maturity.

The body's genetic range modulates all its systems. Genes control the range of physical changes strength training brings—unless drugs override the genetic program. The athlete's physical condition, age, and sex also significantly affect any program's results. That's why two athletes can follow identical programs with markedly different results. Chapters 2 through 4 explore these topics further.

But regardless of how much we change, each of us can apply the physical changes achieved in the weight room to improved sports performance on the field, course, or track.

CHAPTER TWO

STRENGTH TRAINING FOR KIDS

The best time to start strength training is now.

Regardless of your age, strength training can improve your athletic performance. A ten-year-old shot-putter throws farther, a twelve-year-old basketball player jumps higher, an eleven-year-old football player hits harder, and an eight-year-old sprinter runs faster. All young athletes perform *better* after strength training.

Not only will your strength increase, but so will your power and speed—factors instrumental to athletic success. Waiting another month or another year only puts you behind your competitors who already strength-train.

Picking the best program depends on your growth and development. Exercise selection, the number of sets and repetitions, and how often you should train each week depend on your particular growth stage.

Let's explore the differences that age makes in strength-training programs.

WHAT IS NORMAL DEVELOPMENT?

Kids come in all different shapes and sizes, but they follow the same general developmental plan.

After birth, a child's growth rate gradually slows until puberty begins. The child who grew more than two inches during his third year might grow one inch during his tenth. That's normal.

Muscle growth follows the pattern of bone growth, gradually slowing from age two until puberty, at which time muscle mass rapidly increases. In short, muscle and bone retain a constant ratio as the child's system retains a structural balance.

On average, boys are slightly taller and heavier than girls, and grow a little faster. But overall size difference is minor among prepubescents, and athletic performance is similar.

WHAT IS A PREPUBESCENT?

Prepubescent is a technical term for a child. The body has yet to sexually mature in appearance or chemistry, or to produce the genetically programmed hormone surge that initiates transformation into adult size, stature, and strength. That description fits the average child until late elementary or middle school. Size and athletic performance remain the same until puberty begins—at age 12 to 15 years for boys and 10 to 13 years for girls. Girls' earlier entry into puberty often makes them larger than male classmates at this age.

Parents and coaches can spot puberty's onset by noting changes in appearance. Pubic hair, facial hair, testicle enlargement, and a deepening voice mark puberty for boys. Pubic hair and breast development at the onset of menstruation signal puberty for girls. Childhood's end is also roughly defined by the adolescent growth spurt.

The journey from childhood to puberty is a gradual progression. If you need an accurate definition of your child's developmental stage, consult a pediatrician. He or she can quickly determine the individual child's point of development.

WHY DOES THE DEVELOPMENTAL STAGE MATTER?

The developmental stage is significant when designing a strength-training program. Young boys and girls reap the same athletic edge from strength training as athletes in any other age group. But kids' skeletons, nerves, muscles, and emotions are different, so they require programs with precautionary allowances for the ongoing growth process.

IS EMOTIONAL READINESS A FACTOR?

Generally, kids ten and older take to strength training. The immediate strength increases provide a source of accomplishment, enhance self-esteem, and stimulate them to continue training.

But just as adult training programs are inappropriate for a kid's developing body, adult training expectations are inappropriate for the child's psyche. The younger the child, the more unlikely the applicability.

A strength-training program must address the individual child, incorporating his or her attention span, desire, understanding, goals, and reward structure. In psychological terms, those are the child's affective, cognitive, and value-development stages.

Even at the same age, kids have different abilities and temperaments. Children change rapidly, and the readiness for strength training's different elements can come about quickly. The following chart suggests the average child's characteristics and corresponding training; consider them when designing a children's program. But keep in mind that the individual might be ahead of or behind the developmental curve. As parents know, most kids develop intellectually and emotionally according to a standard sequence, but each passes through the stages at a different rate.

Age-Related Characteristics and Weight Training

Age	Characteristics	Implications for Weight Training
Kindergarten and first grade (5–7)	Short attention span Often reckless Constantly active; enjoy rough-and-tumble play Often noisy, exhibitionistic, and attention-demanding	Not ready for weight training
Second, third, and fourth grades (7–10)	Enjoy group activity Like physical contact and games; active Some sports-skills attainment Attention span longer	Rarely ready for weight training (can use body weight as resistance)
Fifth and sixth grades (10–12)	Interested in rules of games Higher interest in sports and sports activity Signs of competitiveness Desire to excel in skill and physical challenges Muscular coordination improving Attention to learning details and technique	Often ready for weight-training skills

IS STRENGTH TRAINING THE SAME AS WEIGHT LIFTING?

Strength training and *weight lifting* are two distinctly different activities sharing a common implement, much as tag and tackle football share the same field and ball. It is important to understand the differences, particularly regarding children.

Strength training is an exercise system designed to increase strength through various set and rep combinations. Prepubescent athletes should begin with sets of at least ten repetitions, using far less weight than if a single, maximum repetition were attempted.

Weight lifting is attempting to lift as heavy a weight as possible, a maximal lift. It's a competitive activity, whether attempting a personal best in the gym or trying to beat the competition on an Olympic platform. Children should not perform maximal lifts except for occasional tests supervised by an experienced adult.

At first glance, the distinction between strength training and weight lifting might seem semantic. However, noting the difference is a vital safety precaution when administering a young athlete's program.

HOW MANY SETS AND REPS?

Research confirms that the following set and rep pattern is both safe and effective for the young athlete. (Chapter 8 will provide a more in-depth explanation about sets and reps.) The incredible prepubescent strength gains cited throughout this book were achieved through the following recommendations:

1. Sports Strength Program exercises: two sets of ten reps per exercise
2. Supplementary exercises: two sets of twelve reps per exercise
3. Returning from a layoff: two sets of fifteen reps per exercise

Prepubescent athletes with at least six months of continuous training respond positively to periodic changes in set/rep patterns. However, in no case should the prepubescent perform fewer than six reps per set, or more than three sets per exercise. The six-rep threshold ensures that the stress will not approach a single-repetition maximum. The three-sets-per-exercise limit ensures that total training volume will remain safe.

HOW MUCH REST BETWEEN WORKOUTS?

Resting two days between workouts allows the child to physically and psychologically re-energize. This means two workouts per week in most cases. If facilities and supervision are available seven days a week, workouts can be slightly more frequent, but in most situations, the child will train on Monday and Thursday or Tuesday and Friday. This will safeguard against overtraining, without impeding strength gains.

IS SUPERVISION NECESSARY?

Strength-training experts overwhelmingly recommend that kids train only under an experienced adult supervisor or coach.

According to both the American Academy of Pediatrics and the National Strength and Conditioning Association, a well-trained supervisor appreciates the physiological differences between adults and children in general structure, hormone production, ossification patterns, recommended exercises, and emotional development. In short, he or she makes strength training safe.

Weight training has proven to be more than safe for children; it also aids injury prevention and enhances athletic performance, as is discussed throughout this chapter.

SHOULD KIDS USE THE SAME EQUIPMENT AS ADULTS?

Most weight-training machines aren't kid-friendly. They are not inherently unsafe, but most simply do not fit the average-size child.

Manufacturers design equipment that fits the greatest potential market. Given that kids are not a large percentage of strength trainers, gym equipment is designed to fit the physical dimensions of an average-size adult. If the kid doesn't fit, the machine can be dangerous, placing strain where it doesn't belong.

Of course, not all machines have a built-in size restriction. For example, the typical squat rack works for any body size. Machines that properly accommodate a kid's body offer convenience, and often allow for easier spotting. There are no plates to load and unload, and nothing to drop. If the machine fits, use it.

ARE FREE WEIGHTS BETTER THAN MACHINES?

Free weights—barbells and dumbbells—are often best for small bodies. They conform to the child's movement rather than forcing the child's body to mimic a large machine's exaggerated motion. Often, free weights duplicate an athletic movement best, helping the strength trainer to adhere to the "specificity" principle (detailed in chapter 3).

Coaches must closely monitor free-weight use, because pulling and thrusting heavy weights produces new concerns. The young strength trainers must maintain balance and proper form, and use spotters for certain lifts.

The most successful training programs use various equipment: free weights and machines. Each piece is carefully chosen to serve the individual athlete's body and sport.

SHOULD KIDS PERFORM THE SAME EXERCISES AS ADULTS?

The most obvious difference between a child's body and an adult's is size, but the skeletal, muscular, and nervous systems' capacities are also different. Respect these differences and select exercises appropriate for the child's body.

The immature body houses an immature nervous system. For example, myelination, a physical change in nerve tissue which increases a nerve impulse or signal's transmission speed, is not complete until sexual maturity. The child, unable to process sensory information as quickly as the adult, cannot perform with the same coordination, balance, agility, and skill.

A child's different skeletal proportions can prevent him or her from executing proper technique, making some exercises inappropriate. The prepubescent's narrower shoulders and shorter arms, for example, increase injury potential to the shoulder girdle and lower back.

When strength, skeletal dimensions, or other considerations preclude certain exercises, safe and effective alternatives are always available. Replacing the squat with the leg press or lunge is one example.

The squat is an excellent lower-body exercise, but it also can lead to back injuries resulting from poor technique. Correct technique depends on strong back and abdominal muscles, which the child new to strength training usually lacks. But the squat can be effectively replaced. The leg press and lunge target the same muscle groups as the squat—the legs and hips—without demanding as much back and abdominal strength. Alternative exercises provide the prepubescent with a safe and effective lower-body workout. The leg press supports the back while targeting the lower-body

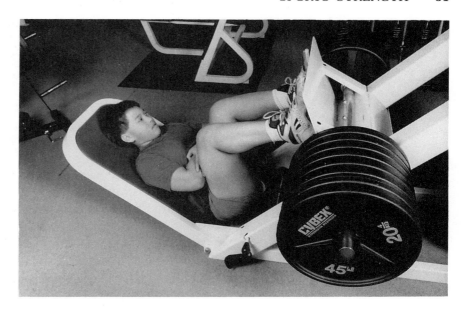

Leg presses—not squats—effectively stress a young athlete's legs. This twelve-year-old is leg-pressing 1,000 pounds.

muscles. The lunge encourages a straight back while targeting the lower body. Both avoid overloading an unprepared back. The squat can be incorporated into workouts later in the young athlete's career, when back and abdominal strength are sufficient to meet the challenge.

A final point on exercise selection: Overhead lifts are not recommended for a child. Performing the new skill with an unprepared back invites injury. Kids should train for a year, including back exercises, before performing overhead lifts.

This book's strength-training programs recommend kids' exercises as part of each sport-specific program. Those selections are geared for the developing body.

HOW STRONG CAN KIDS GET?

Several scientific journals report prepubescent strength increases as high as 50 percent after only nine weeks of strength training. Other researchers have correlated improved vertical jump and long-jump performance after a six-week strength-training program. *The Journal of Orthopedic and Sports Physical Therapy* put it best: "Recent investigations overwhelmingly support significant strength gains in prepubescents as a result of weight training."

WHAT MAKES A KID'S BODY STRONGER?

When scientists study adult males, they find that muscle size increases when strength increases. In other words, a stronger muscle is a bigger muscle. Because of that research, scientists were puzzled that both boys and girls increase dramatically in strength without increasing muscle size. In fact, studies found as much as a 100 percent strength increase with no measurable muscle-size change. What caused the strength gains?

A child's strength gains result from learning to use *more* muscle when needed. The nervous system learns to signal additional muscle cells to participate in a push or pull; this improved cooperation between muscles and nerves is called neural adaptation. Neural adaptation's intricacies are not completely understood. What's certain is that strength training greatly increases a child's strength, which improves athletic performance. For a deeper understanding of this phenomenon, read about neural adaptations on page 18.

DO RAPID STRENGTH GAINS CONTINUE?

After fast gains during an introductory strength-training period, prepubescents' gains plateau. The reason is the same as that for any experienced weight lifter: Neural adaptations produce the fast, early gains. Further appreciations rely more on actual muscle growth.

The prepubescent athlete faces an enormously difficult task when attempting to grow bigger muscles. The reason is the low levels of testosterone, the sex-specific hormone necessary for growing bigger muscles. Little research is available on the prepubescent's long-term strength-gain prospects; after all, if a prepubescent begins training at ten, "long term" could be anywhere from one to three years before the young person enters puberty. However, anecdotal reports and personal observation suggest that strength gains *do* continue through prepuberty. The rate decreases after the introductory period, but absolute strength increases slowly with little additional muscle size. However, strength gains may be attributable to the pituitary's increased growth-hormone production during intense training, or to continued neural adaptations. The precise adaptive mechanism is not important; the prepubescent's strength does increase through weight training.

CAN KIDS GROW BIG MUSCLES?

The research community's opinion is that strength training cannot increase a kid's muscle size; however, the studies conducted to date have been too short to decide the issue. After all, muscle growth takes time and intense effort, even with adult males who have the advantage of extensive muscle-building hormones.

Male hormone—testosterone—undoubtedly helps increase

muscle quantity. However, other factors also influence the muscle mass increase, as evidenced by the natural growth that boys and girls experience from birth to puberty. One such factor is growth hormone, which stimulates both muscle and bone growth.

Interestingly, boys and girls who strength-train have more growth hormone production, which *might* culminate in more muscle mass.

As a practical matter, it is unlikely that a child will grow big muscles. Size gains won't come until puberty for boys, and perhaps never for girls. Kids can't look like Arnold Schwarzenegger from strength training, but they can become stronger, better athletes.

DOES STRENGTH TRAINING HARM BONES?

Contrary to a popular conception, strength training does not stunt a child's growth. Not one example in the medical and scientific literature supports the notion that strength training limits a child's ultimate skeletal length. Let's set the record straight.

Numerous, well-documented, sports-science studies unequivocally conclude that a properly designed strength-training program has no adverse impact on a child's skeletal development. A study published in *The Journal of Orthopedic and Sports Physical Therapy* is typical of scientific results that find "no damage to bone, epiphyses and growth tissue" from such training.

In fact, strength training is safer than all the sports found in an average school athletic program. Statistically, young athletes are more likely to suffer skeletal injuries competing in basketball, soccer, running, football, baseball, wrestling, or gymnastics than from engaging in a strength-training program.

If you're a kid or a coach involved with strength training, you're bound to encounter questions about bone injuries. Let's look at the relationship between weight training and two injury types: acute and chronic.

Acute Skeletal Injuries

Acute injury is that resulting from a single trauma, blow, or collision—the type that a cross-block, hard landing, or a jab in the eye produces.

In the past, a misconceived fear existed that children who strength-trained risked acute injury to their growth plates, but far more growth-plate fractures take place on the playground. A few cases of growth-plate fractures among prepubescent strength trainers have been documented, but they happened during overhead lifts or when the child attempted maximum lifts—factors that double the danger. Imagine a single all-out effort gone awry: The child loses control and is hit by the falling weights. In this scenario, anyone—adult or child—is likely to become injured.

Supervisors must accept that children, especially beginners, should focus on technique, and eliminate maximal overhead lifts from the young person's program. Safely balancing a very heavy weight above the head requires technique, coordination, and concentration that is difficult even for older, more experienced lifters.

Chronic Injuries

Chronic injuries result from repeated blows or continuous stress. One example is a stress fracture resulting from running too much on hard surfaces.

The repeated small stresses of athletic movements, as opposed to a one-time maximal stress, have caused skeletal problems for some young athletes. Most notably, "Little League shoulder" results from the repeated throwing motion's stress. But strength-training several hours each week has demonstrated no damaging effect on growth and development. To put it in perspective, twenty minutes of a basketball scrimmage subjects growing leg bones to more potentially damaging forces than *two weeks* of strength-training workouts.

Providing that they follow a program designed for kids, young athletes can strength-train to improve sports performance without worrying that the skeletal system will be harmed.

Positive Effects on Bone

Strength training increases the child's bone strength, reducing the risk of injury during athletics.

The stress of exercise, particularly strength training, increases the bone's structural integrity (strength). In fact, the adaptation of bone, muscle, and the circulatory system is the exercise's sought-after result.

Bone is constantly remodeling throughout childhood, the density changing in response to applied mechanical forces, primarily muscular contractions. Strength training, by increasing the mechanical forces on the bone, increases bone thickness and density. A physiological process captures bone-building minerals moving through the bloodstream; once captured, the minerals, mostly calcium and phosphorus, layer the outside and pack remaining space inside the bone. The increased thickness and density increases the bone's structural strength, which makes it better able to absorb shock, and accommodate the stronger muscle contractions of athletics.

Designing a child's program requires that coaches appreciate the physical and emotional differences that separate children from one another as well as from adults.

Given an age-appropriate program, children reap the same benefits as adults: the improved strength, muscular endurance, speed, power, and flexibility that positively affect athletic performance. And a strength-trained athlete is far less likely to have sports-specific injuries.

Strength training is safe and effective, but the intensity and complexity of the program should depend on the child's desire and ability, not on the adult in the background.

CHAPTER THREE

EARLY ADOLESCENCE:
Strength Training and the Growth Spurt

The one word that describes early adolescence is "change." Leafing through a family picture album, we see a little boy and girl become young adults with the flip of a page.

And more than the outward appearance changes. Internally, the body's chemistry becomes more adult. Bones and muscles grow and the emotions swirl.

Boys and girls experience common changes, but there are also sex-specific transformations. For example, all early adolescents gain muscle mass, but boys gain more. That's part of the genetic blueprint that defines males and females, as are the skeletal dimensions and hormone distribution.

Early adolescence is also the time that many young people first strength-train. On the one hand, it's the best time to start, because studies indicate that training will never again produce such rapid results. On the other hand, it's also a time for caution: Ongoing physical changes—coupled with the adolescent's exuberance and inexperience—can result in injury.

Coaches or supervisors must take care to design a training program that protects the early adolescent's rapidly changing body. Hidden or visible, structural or chemical, the young person's internal and external changes must be factored in.

The training programs suggested in this book reflect the early adolescent's unique qualities. The following material encapsulates those recommendations' basis.

DO EARLY ADOLESCENTS REQUIRE SUPERVISION?

Common sense dictates that the supervision level depends on the young athlete's psychological maturity, physical stage, and experience. Don't use age as the guide. Although a small fraction of a life span, early adolescence is a whirlwind of psychological change. What is too little supervision one month becomes too much the next. As a rule of thumb, be overcautious.

Supervisors must provide the experience, particularly regarding technique and weight selection. Choose exercises and weights according to the athlete's coordination, experience, physical condition, and skeletal development. Don't allow a younger athlete to "see if I can do it" after watching an older athlete train.

DO CHILDREN ENTER ADOLESCENCE AT THE SAME AGE?

Early adolescence, or puberty, begins as the endocrine system releases a surge of sex-specific hormones. This happens according to an inherited genetic plan, which is why children begin adolescence at slightly different ages. The normal child enters puberty at between ten and fifteen years of age.

WHAT IS THE ADOLESCENT GROWTH SPURT?

The *growth spurt* is a rapid height increase at puberty's onset. This "flood" often occurs during middle school as legs outgrow pants. Boys' growth spurts average four inches a year, and girls' average three inches.

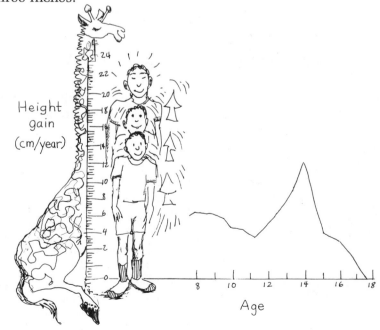

Early adolescence ends when the growth spurt stops. At this point, the adolescent can begin training more as an adult.

SHOULD EARLY ADOLESCENTS AVOID MAXIMAL WEIGHTS?

According to the American Academy of Pediatrics, young athletes should not lift maximal weights until they are sixteen—the statistical age at which the growth spurt is probably complete.

The skeleton's growth centers (growth plates) are presumed to be particularly vulnerable during the growth spurt, and two types of skeletal injuries could result from using maximum weights at this time. One, of course, is dropping the weight on the body. This happens more often than you might imagine, because of inexperience or trying to lift too heavy a weight.

The second injury type results from accumulated growth-plate microtraumas. As the name implies, a microtrauma is a small injury. While not a problem in and of itself, small injuries add up to more serious injury. The medical argument assumes that lifting near-maximal weights produces growth-plate microtraumas. Accumulated, they might retard the bone's natural growth and development.

The growth spurt is complete by fifteen for most boys and thirteen for most girls. But that's only an average; a broad individual range exists.

Since a young person's genetic program determines when the growth spurt begins, the age at which it is safe to train with maximal weight varies. Heavy squats may be unsafe for a tenth-grade football player who hasn't completed his growth spurt, whereas a seventh grader with adequate experience might be ready for an adult training program. Whether or not to use maximal weights depends on skeletal maturity and experience.

HOW MANY SETS AND REPS DURING THE GROWTH SPURT?

The priorities are simple: natural growth first, strength training second. The program should not interfere with the ongoing growth spurt. With that in mind, review the following recommendations:

1. Sports Strength Program exercises: two sets of ten reps per exercise
2. Supplementary exercises: two sets of twelve reps per exercise
3. Returning from a layoff: two sets of fifteen reps per exercise

Like experienced prepubescent strength athletes, early adolescents respond positively to periodic changes in set-rep patterns. However, early adolescents should never perform fewer than six reps per set, or more than three sets per exercise. The six-rep threshold ensures that the stress will not approach a single-repetition maximum. The limit of three sets per exercise ensures that total training volume will not deter natural growth.

HOW MUCH REST BETWEEN WORKOUTS?

As a practical matter, resting two days between workouts allows the early adolescent to physically and psychologically re-energize. This pattern allows for two workouts per week in most cases. If the training facilities and supervision are available seven days a week, workouts can be slightly more frequent, but in most situations, the young athlete will train on Monday and Thursday, or Tuesday and Friday. Two workouts per week will increase strength without impeding physical growth.

WHY FOCUS ON THE LOWER BACK AND ABDOMEN?

Many trainers and researchers recommend a year of lower-back and abdomen strengthening before including squats and overhead lifts in a program. Early adolescence is an excellent time for specialized back and abdomen training, permitting a smooth transition into squats and overhead lifts after the growth spurt has ended. It's also a great time to build good training habits. As you'll see later in the book, the lower back and abdomen are the areas most neglected by older athletes. Without strengthening these areas, power generated by the legs cannot travel through the torso to reach the shoulders and arms.

DO MALES AND FEMALES DEVELOP DIFFERENT SKELETAL PROPORTIONS?

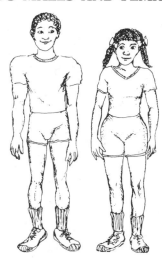

During the growth spurt, adult males and females acquire different skeletal proportions. These differences manifest during early adolescence and affect training capacity. The coach can no longer expect the same results from men and women executing the same strength-training program.

During early adolescence, boys' bones grow comparatively longer and wider. The boy's wider shoulders can hold more muscle, and create a mechanical advantage through which that muscle can exert greater force. Throughout life, the sexes' strength differences are greatest at the shoulders because of early-adolescent skeletal developments.

A girl's hips grow comparatively wider during the early-adolescent growth spurt, and her legs remain relatively shorter. This increases the mechanical advantage during lower-body movements, making her closer to males in lower-body strength than in upper-body strength.

The different skeletal proportions prevent the adolescent or adult female from correctly executing several popular exercises developed by men.

DOES THE GROWTH SPURT DISTURB FLEXIBILITY?

Boys and girls grow up before filling out, because the muscle-tissue increase lags behind the skeletal-growth increase. These different growth rates contribute to the early adolescent's lack of flexibility in the hamstrings and lower back, particularly for boys.

Hamstring inflexibility contributes to a *weak link* at the lower back. The tight hamstrings below the hips combine with unequal growth rates of the vertebrae and spinal erectors above the hips, producing an exaggerated forward curvature of the lower spine. This exaggerated curvature (lordosis) may subject the back to increased injury risk, especially when part of an immature skeleton.

Not all athletes experience lordosis during early adolescence, and flexibility exercises, especially for the hamstrings, can prevent it or alleviate an existing problem. Still, it's a factor to consider when prescribing or following an exercise prescription for early adolescents.

WHY ARE RESULTS FASTER FOR BOYS?

Strength training's results—the amount the muscle cell grows—are tied to the amount of testosterone that circulates through the body.

Male hormone (testosterone) and *female hormone* (estrogen) are not mutually exclusive to males or females; every body has some of each. But the male's body has more testosterone and the female's body has more estrogen.

Testosterone is vital to muscle growth because it turns on genetic switches within the cell's nucleus, activating the production of protein—the primary building block for new muscle tissue. Hence, the body with more testosterone is capable of building more muscle.

For the male, adolescence's onset causes testosterone production to surge to at least a thousand percent greater than during childhood, and at least a thousand percent more than the testosterone a normal adolescent female produces. Testosterone and strength training combine to produce muscle growth and strength far greater than is possible for the adolescent or adult female; in general, her muscles build very slowly.

Testosterone is not the only factor causing a difference in male and female growth rates, but it is a major ingredient. That's why female athletes taking steroids (synthetic derivatives of testosterone) become much more muscular than competitors who don't.

Adolescent males also experience strength increases. When beginning a program, both sexes experience rapid initial strength gains resulting from neural adaptations (see chapter 1). Beyond those early neural adaptations, though, strength gains depend mostly on increased muscle size, which depends on testosterone. For the adolescent male, strength training and testosterone produce muscle growth and strength that is possible earlier. For the adolescent female, strength training increases size and strength, but not with the same rapidity or absolute dimensions available to the adolescent male. Her natural testosterone supply limits her adaptational response to training, a sex-based inequity.

DO STEROIDS STOP THE GROWTH SPURT?

Steroids don't just build muscle, they affect every tissue in the body. Chapter 6 deals with the facts concerning steroids, which are chemically and functionally similar to testosterone. There is no doubt that steroids increase strength, muscle mass, and sports performance, but there are potential side effects that can be very dangerous.

The body's endocrine system is a finely tuned distribution network, regulating the release of naturally produced testosterone in harmony with many other hormones. The system operates through a series of genetically programmed checks and balances. The amount of natural testosterone released by the endocrine system contributes to normal skeletal development, and is a necessary ingredient for growth.

Steroids, on the other hand, flood the body with testosterone (or testosterone substitutes). A synthetic oversupply of one ingredient disrupts the genetic program's balance. The growth plates' testosterone-sensitive receptors are saturated—a signal for the cartilaginous growth plates to fuse into bone. Once this occurs, the skeleton stops growing. The degree of fusion and resulting loss in mature height depends somewhat on the steroid consumption's quantity and duration. What's more, steroids have the same effect on both males and females.

Early adolescence is a time of rapid structural, chemical, and emotional change, when training requires experienced supervision. As a result, coaches, teachers, and parents must calculate the ongoing growth process into the training program's design.

The next level is adult training. Early adolescence should lay a foundation of good training habits that will carry the athlete through the rest of his or her athletic career.

CHAPTER FOUR

ADVANCED TRAINING FOR LATE TEENS AND ADULTS

Advanced training is a *personal* program designed for your body. Bodybuilding and weight-training books often dictate one "right" way to train, but the more specific the advice, the more suspicious you should be. Several decades of research has not produced a strength-training program that's right for everyone.

When you shop for a new pair of running shoes, you buy the size that fits you, not your favorite athlete. In the same way, your strength training must suit your body, time constraints, current condition, recuperative abilities, and your relative strengths and weaknesses. One size doesn't fit all.

Imagine your friends' different body types. Each has a unique combination of bone lengths, tendon attachments, hormone production, and thousands of other physical variations that affect performance. That's why individuals in any athletic group achieve different results from identical training programs.

You might be part of a team, and even look like the player standing next to you, but your body is unique. Your workout must be individually designed. With that in mind, use this book as a framework. Modify. Experiment.

Several chapters in this book are devoted to how and why strength training changes your body. The better you understand those specifics, the better you can synthesize a personally tailored training program. The remainder of this chapter combines practical advice and scientific fact. Choose according to your body and your goals. Think for yourself.

WHEN CAN A TEEN BEGIN ADVANCED TRAINING?

Sixteen is the most frequently recommended age for beginning advanced programs—those with the same design latitude as an adult's. Statistically, the growth spurt is complete by this age. The young person is now less vulnerable to muscular and skeletal injuries, so there is less need to limit the workout because of ongoing growth and development.

A presumption exists that the average sixteen-year-old is also emotionally and intellectually responsible. After all, if you're mature enough for a driver's license, you can follow a weight room's safety rules.

WHAT PROGRAM ELEMENTS CAN BE MODIFIED?

All strength-training programs can be divided into six elements: sets and reps, exercise choice, exercise order, rest periods, training volume, and loads (amount of weight). Changing any one of these variables affects the program's outcome. For example, imagine the different results between one set of six repetitions with a heavy weight, and another comprised of sixty repetitions with a light weight. The low-rep, heavy-weight combination is better at building strength; the high-rep, light-weight combination is better for muscular endurance.

Conceptually, that's all there is to shifting variables. Exercise selection, sequence, volume, and rest periods are just as easily manipulated to change the training program's outcome. In practice, that might mean choosing incline presses rather than bench presses, leg curls before squats, sets and reps totaling fifty thousand rather than a hundred thousand pounds, and two days' rest rather than one between workouts. Gear the schedule to your individual needs, and review the training variables by referring to chapter 8 as you fine-tune your workout.

HOW WILL I KNOW THE RIGHT COMBINATION?

Try several different combinations over a period of months, and keep a training log, comparing the results. If the findings are inconclusive, at least you've added variety to your training, an important stimulus to increased strength.

One caveat. Although you're experimenting, use common sense. *Avoid extremes.* Stay between one and ten reps, for one to ten sets, selecting the appropriate load (see chapter 7).

CAN BIGGER MUSCLES BE A DISADVANTAGE?

Bigger muscles are what lure most males to weight training. Yet if the muscles aren't necessary to a sport, or if the muscle mass interferes with technique, then the growth is a disadvantage.

Imagine a high jumper with twenty extra pounds of muscle not involved in the jumping movement. That's a twenty-pound handicap that must be lifted over the bar. Or imagine a boxer with pectoral muscles so large that they interfere with his punching technique. You get the picture.

Muscle for muscle's sake is a mistake for the athlete. Be specific in your gains, building only where it will enhance your physical performance. Excess baggage drains energy, flexibility, and speed.

WHY ARE LEGS THE FIRST PRIORITY?

"First you lose your legs. Then you lose your friends."

—Willie Pep, world champion boxer

"His legs are gone" is jargon that usually refers to a thirty-five- or forty-year-old athlete's loss of leg power, but can just as easily describe many late teens and athletes in their early twenties.

If time is scarce, train your legs—each throw, punch, thrust, swing, jump, or step begins with them. Increased leg strength adds power to every move, whether it's the first step toward the basket or the last step toward first base.

Leg work seems less attractive than upper-body work because, unfortunately, leg size and strength aren't valued by beginning weight trainers. The legs are far more important to the average athlete's success, but early habits are hard to break.

The older the athlete, the more important the legs become. Without intervention, maximum natural strength gradually weakens after the mid-twenties, accompanied by a corresponding speed and power decline. On the other hand, strength training *increases* speed and power, extending competitive performance.

WHY DO STRENGTH GAINS SLOW?

Beginners are blessed with rapid strength increases. Numerous studies, using inexperienced men, women, and children as subjects, report strength gains of 50 percent or more after twelve to twenty weeks of training. As the beginner accumulates experience, though, the advancement slows. World weight-lifting champions—the most experienced strength-trained athletes— struggle for a two-percent increase over a year. What causes this disproportion?

The answer depends on strength training's predominant physical adaptation. The beginner's body adapts to training stress primarily by teaching more existing muscle to take part in the action. These are the neural adaptations discussed in chapter 1.

Neural adaptations are rapid and impressive, projecting the inexperienced athlete on an upward spiral of strength gains. But the pool of potential neural adaptations is soon exhausted. After several months, the beginner gains strength at a rate closer to the experienced lifter's. All the muscle fibers that a lift could recruit were brought in long before, so additional strength increases require building more muscle; as experienced strength trainers will attest, this is a slow process. A final factor is that experienced athletes operate closer to their genetic limits—much less adaptation is *possible*.

Judging the beginner's gains against the experienced strength athlete's is like comparing apples and oranges: neural adaptations versus more muscle. The experienced strength trainer's increases come slowly, but any successful athlete will tell you that the extra work was worth it—that additional strength is often what separates victory from defeat.

WHY AREN'T FEMALE ATHLETES AS STRONG?

Female strength athletes follow the same path as males—rapidly gaining initial strength due to neural adaptations rather than increased muscle size, with the gains leveling off when the neural adaptations pool is exhausted. Studies subjecting males and females to the same strength-training program, however, find that the females' strength rate increases are far less than males'. Absolute strength and muscle hypertrophy also are less.

Several gender-related physiological factors are assumed responsible for these differences, including that males have more circulating testosterone, and that their muscle cells also have more nuclei, the genetic storehouses necessary for synthesizing muscle-building protein.

The adult female's absolute strength is approximately two-thirds that of a male's after following programs of the same relative intensity. The difference is less in lower-body strength and greater in upper-body strength, but in all areas, the female's body is substantially weaker.

A female is not automatically weaker than a male, though. It is not uncommon to find a strength-trained female 100 percent stronger than the average untrained male when both are tested in certain lifts.

How females adapt to strength training is of little practical importance. Just remember that strength training substantially increases the female's strength, which can then improve sports performance.

WHY DON'T FEMALES GET AS MUSCULAR?

The female athlete can grow muscle, but having less testosterone to build and maintain more muscle tissue inhibits her growth rate. As a result, the female must train much harder and longer than the average male to add the same percentage of muscle, and the mass possible is genetically limited.

There are exceptions, however. Female bodybuilding's rise has produced a few very muscular women, but the available studies aren't conclusive. These women may have an atypical genetic predisposition to muscle growth; others ingest anabolic steroids [see chapter 6, "Steroids"]. Evidence that only a few females grow big muscles suggests that it is an abnormal adaptation.

Most females' long-term prospects for maintaining big muscles are slim. It is also unlikely that a normal female can ever approach an equivalently trained male's strength. Inherent, sex-defined physiological parameters distinguish the muscle-development rate, absolute growth, and absolute strength.

In conclusion, the female's muscles *do* grow bigger and stronger from strength training, and the mechanisms are the same as a male's. However, the female's growth and strength gains are *relatively* limited because of sex-defined physiological factors.

DO *MORE* CELLS OR *BIGGER* CELLS INCREASE SIZE?

At issue is *how* muscles grow bigger. Does growth result from an increase in the number of cells (hyperplasia) or an increase in the existing cells' size (hypertrophy)?

Exercise physiologists believe that hypertrophy is muscle growth's primary mechanism. As noted in chapter 1, individual cells adapt to strength training by increasing the quantity of myofibrils, a muscle contraction's functional machinery. More myofibrils, and their accompanying cellular support material, increase the cell's volume. As the individual cells increase in size, the overall muscle gets bigger. Whether hyperplasia accounts for even a minor size increase will be decided as more research takes place.

"It's what you learn after you know it all that counts."

—John Wooden, UCLA basketball coach

Advanced strength training is a personal project. Try many different workouts before settling on what's best for you, and continue to adapt the program to fit your needs.

Familiarize yourself with how your body works, and always train safely. When in doubt, seek expert advice, but you are the ultimate authority. You're in charge of your body.

Try the different set-rep, rest, and exercise formats discussed in chapter 6. They not only vary your workouts, but also extend the range of your muscles' adaptational response.

Good luck with your experiment!

CHAPTER FIVE

FOOD: FUELING THE BODY

What to eat and how much: that's all there is to understanding nutrition. Strength training stimulates muscle growth, but food supplies the building blocks.

Let's begin with how much food the athlete needs.

HOW MUCH FOOD?

Athletes come in all sizes, and need different amounts of food. The *Los Angeles Times* reported that the smallest participant at the 1991 Sports Festival was sixty-pound gymnast Amy Chow. The largest was 370-pound Mark Henry, a super-heavyweight weight lifter.

The average adult eats eleven hundred pounds of food each year. The average athlete eats two times that much. That's twice the calorie amount and double the bill at the supermarket. Why?

Because athletes exercise more, they need more food for more energy. For example, a female writer sitting in front of a computer needs about 1,800 calories a day to talk, write, and take the occasional walk to the refrigerator. If she's pregnant, she needs another 300 to 500 calories for the growing baby. A female distance runner, on the other hand, needs about 5,500 calories a day to satisfy her additional energy demands—that's three times the writer's food to satisfy triple the energy demands.

Most active people's caloric demands fall somewhere between the writer's and the distance runner's, but the first factor separating athletes from nonathletes is now apparent: They require more food to fuel greater energy expenditures, and probably have thinner wallets too.

DO AGE AND GENDER MAKE A DIFFERENCE?

Statisticians tell us that age and sex affect food consumption, but their evaluations are based on the average person—not the hard-core athlete.

For example, a moderately active adult male needs about 3,000 kilocalories a day, whereas a moderately active fourteen-year-old girl needs 2,500. However, if the man were a construction worker and the girl were a distance runner, they would need 3,500 and 5,500 calories a day, respectively. Age and sex do not control food needs—size and activity level do. The growth period—about one-seventh of a person's life—does require more nutrients, but those minor variations are easily met by eating more.

WHAT IS THE RIGHT AMOUNT OF FOOD?

Exercise uses energy derived from food eaten last night, last week, or even last year. The balance between how much you eat and how much you use determines whether you're eating the right amount.

You already know the rule of thumb for calculating energy balance: If you eat too much, you'll gain weight. If you eat too little, you'll lose weight. Beyond that, don't worry about it. You don't need to perpetually count calories; just occasionally consult the scale. That might sound too simple, but it's really the most practical monitor.

SHOULD ATHLETES FEAR A NEGATIVE ENERGY BALANCE?

Energy has to come from somewhere. If the food consumed doesn't satisfy a person's energy needs, the body feeds on itself. An extreme example is the starvation that millions of third-world people endure through famine. Without food, the body ravishes its muscle tissue to maintain a subsistent energy level as long as it can. Strength continually drops, making each step more difficult than the last.

In less dramatic ways, the same process happens to the undernourished athlete. First the body will eat its own fat, which is fine if the athlete isn't trying to gain strength. But after the fat is consumed, the body starts feeding on its own muscle.

CAN ATHLETES GAIN MUSCLE WHILE LOSING WEIGHT?

Athletes on a weight-loss diet can't gain muscle, regardless of how hard they train, because the negative energy balance prevents muscle growth.

When energy is scarce, the body allocates it in order of importance. The first priority is to keep the body alive; the second priority is to maintain *all* existing tissue. Building additional muscle tissue is well down the list.

Muscle won't grow without strength training *and* enough food to produce a positive energy balance.

CAN ATHLETES ADD MUSCLE WITHOUT ADDING FAT?

No; a positive energy balance increases fat as well as muscle. That doesn't mean that an ounce of fat is added with every ounce of new muscle. Nor does it mean that the new muscle cannot be retained as fat is lost later.

Most extra food will be converted into muscle if the strength-training program's demands are sufficiently stressful, but the body's homeostatic balancing mechanism insists that a little fat goes along. The fat content might increase only 5 percent with sixty pounds of added muscle.

CAN FAT BE LOST WITHOUT LOSING MUSCLE?

You won't perpetually wear a spare tire. The athlete can rid the body of added fat while retaining added muscle.

Although significant muscle cannot be *gained* during a weight-loss diet, it can be *maintained* during moderate weight loss, since the body depletes fat stores before the body feeds on existing muscle tissue.

Make sure you eat enough for maintenance *and* growth. You can always lose the extra fat.

WHAT IS A WELL-BALANCED DIET?

A well-balanced diet supplies enough nutrients to satisfy the body's needs, allowing it to repair, replace, and build tissue. Athletics demand ongoing supplies of basic nutrients in the right mix and amount, including vitamins, minerals, proteins, fats, carbohydrates, and water.

Too little protein, even with adequate food volume, results in muscle loss; so does excess protein with inadequate carbohydrates, or lots of fat with too little protein. Balance is as important as quantity.

WHAT'S THE CARBOHYDRATE/PROTEIN/FAT BALANCE?

A balanced diet contains about 15 percent protein, 60 percent carbohydrates, and 25 percent fat. For a sedentary person consuming 1,800 calories daily, that would provide 68 grams of protein, 270 grams of carbohydrates, and 50 grams of fat.

What about the distance runner who consumes 5,500 calories daily? That athlete should take in 206 grams of protein, 825 grams of carbohydrates, and 153 grams of fat.

At first glance, that's a lot of protein for a 130-pound person. But long-distance running requires ongoing physical maintenance. Moving the longest leg muscles requires the most energy output, and the body takes a beating as it pounds the pavement.

WHY AN ONGOING BALANCED DIET?

As noted before, an unbalanced diet can prevent muscle growth and even cause muscle loss. Here are more facts important to the strength-training athlete:

The body has 639 muscles, 206 bones, and millions of nerves; every cell contains proteins. Without consistant protein supplies, cell growth and maintenance would rapidly cease. Strength training would produce negative results—the body will maintain tissue throughout the body before it repairs trained tissue.

Carbohydrates are the primary source of *immediate* energy, providing the fuel that allows protein to do its job. Without a moderate carbohydrate supply, protein cannot build and maintain muscle.

Fats are part of every cell. Two fatty acids, linoleic and arachidonic, are essential, and retaining fat-soluble vitamins requires fat consumption. Don't ignore this very real need.

Vitamins are the body's catalyst in numerous chemical reactions. Minerals take part in enzyme and hormone production, give structure to teeth and blood, and regulate muscle contractions.

These are just a few ways the strength-training athlete relies on a well-balanced diet.

HOW IS A WELL-BALANCED DIET DESIGNED?

According to the U.S. Department of Agriculture, eating a well-balanced diet is as easy as following their food-selection plan.

The basic plan suggests that you select foods from five groups:

1. Bread, cereal, rice, and pasta
2. Vegetables
3. Fruits
4. Milk, yogurt, and cheese
5. Meat, poultry, fish, dried beans, eggs, and nuts

IS THE USDA PLAN ADEQUATE?

Is a well-balanced diet common in America? A 1991 Cornell University study showed that 48 percent of New York City schoolchildren had eaten no vegetables the previous day.

Research indicates that it is, although many athletes go one step further and eat a broader range of foods than recommended by the USDA plan. The plan is not necessarily wrong, but nutritional guidelines are constantly fluctuating.

Broadening your food range simply means eating a greater variety within a given group. For example, rather than eating spinach and corn, consume the same total calories with smaller servings of spinach, corn, peas, green beans, and squash. The rationale is that you'll meet as yet unrecognized nutritional needs.

When counting vitamins and minerals, try to alternate sources, ensuring that you absorb the intended amount. How much of a given nutrient can be absorbed varies with the food. For example, iron from plants is absorbed less efficiently than iron from animals.

Many athletes also take moderate-dosage vitamin/mineral pills as insurance. The premise is that the pill will supply nutrients that the USDA plan doesn't. That's okay.

DO STRENGTH-TRAINING ATHLETES REQUIRE MORE PROTEIN?

Gyms have bred many strange diets. Decades of bodybuilders and weight lifters ate *enormous* quantities of protein, thinking it necessary to build strength and muscle mass. Some ate five pounds of meat each day and washed it down with protein-powder milk shakes.

Strength-training athletes do need more protein than sedentary people, but not in the quantities these bodybuilders advocated.

Protein recommendations are based on body weight. Whereas the nonathlete should consume a half-gram of protein for every pound of body weight, the strength-training athlete should consume *three-fourths of a gram* for every pound of body weight. The athlete needs the added protein for extra muscle-tissue growth and maintenance.

DO PROTEIN REQUIREMENTS FLUCTUATE?

Yes. As training intensity increases, so does the body's need for protein to build and repair tissue.

It's well-known that the body gains or loses fat depending on the balance between calories consumed and energy expended. But the body also has a net gain or net loss of protein, depending on the ongoing balance between consumption and use. Scientists can measure protein levels by monitoring the body's consumption and excretion of nitrogen, a primary element of all protein molecules. A positive nitrogen balance means more muscle has been packed onto the frame, whereas a negative nitrogen balance indicates muscle loss.

But athletes need not worry. Providing you stick to the 15 percent protein/60 percent carbohydrate/25 percent fat ratio, the extra protein comes as part of the food package needed to fuel intense training.

ARE PROTEIN SUPPLEMENTS NECESSARY?

Carl Lewis has maintained a strict vegetarian diet throughout a career that has included a world record in the 100 meters.

No special supplements or special foods are needed. Though the athlete needs enough protein to repair existing muscle tissue and build new tissue, these expanded requirements are satisfied by eating more food and retaining the protein/carbohydrate/fat ratio.

Earlier in the chapter, we noted that a balanced 1,800-calorie diet supplied about 68 grams of protein—adequate for the average-size sedentary person. The same-size athlete, eating twice as many calories to satisfy increased energy demands of training and competition, consumes 135 grams of protein. That's plenty.

Two thoughts should direct the athlete's nutritional plan: energy balance, and the nutrient ratio 15 percent protein, 60 percent carbohydrate, 25 percent fat.

Some of what the athlete eats builds strength and muscle, but only when the food provides a positive energy balance and a proper mix of nutrients.

Training and these simple nutritional facts will go a long way toward making you a champion.

CHAPTER SIX

STEROIDS

HISTORICAL OVERVIEW

1935 Testosterone first isolated.

1942 German troops use anabolic steroids to increase strength and aggressiveness.

1954 Male and female Soviet athletes reportedly use steroids to increase mass and power.

1956 Olga Fikotova Connolly, an Olympic discus thrower, says: "There is no way in the world a woman nowadays, in the throwing events . . . can break the record unless she is on steroids."

1988 Ben Johnson is stripped of his 100-meter Olympic gold medal when his post-race drug test contains steroids.

1991 Steroid possession becomes a federal crime in the United States, with a maximum one-year prison penalty and a minimum $1,000 fine.

In 1955, Dr. John Ziegler, then physician for the U.S. national weight-lifting team, joined forces with Ciba Pharmaceuticals to design the first man-made muscle-building steroid, Dianabol. His interest followed reports that Soviet athletes—at that time the American sports establishment's archrivals—were making amazing progress by injecting themselves with testosterone. Dr. Ziegler experimented with low doses of Dianabol on a small group of elite weight lifters. As he had hoped, the lifters excelled.

After several years, steroid use spread to swimmers, football players, throwers, and runners. The *Journal of Sports Medicine* surveyed twenty track-and-field athletes and weight lifters, and reported that nineteen had taken steroids in preparation for the 1968 Olympic Games.

Although steroids are a male hormone derivative, steroid use wasn't restricted to men. When quizzed about the deep voices of the East German 1976 Olympic team's female swimmers, the coach replied, "We have come here to swim, not sing."

In a 1988 interview with *The New York Times*, Dr. Robert Voy, then the United States Olympic Committee's chief medical officer, stated that a majority of Olympic athletes trained with steroids.

Trickling downward, steroid use spread like an epidemic on the American sports scene, hitting the colleges, then high schools, and finally the junior high schools. What Dr. Ziegler started as a small, controlled experiment had grown into a firestorm.

DANGER SKYROCKETS AS DOSAGES INCREASE

When widespread steroid use began thirty years ago, there were no laws banning steroids for enhanced athletic performance. Family doctors routinely prescribed steroids when requested. The doctors weren't overly concerned: In a *prescribed dosage*, under medical supervision, steroids weren't thought to risk a young athlete's health.

In reality, patients often ignored the prescriptions. Ignorant that serious side effects might result, many athletes thought that if a little is good, more must be better. Dr. Ziegler, in *Death of an Athlete*, recalls finding that his small group of weight lifters was "taking far in excess of this [prescribed low dosage] behind my back and developing all sorts of medical pathologies."

People in gyms across the country offered homespun advice on amounts and brands. The result was predictable: Athletes loaded up on steroids, as much as one hundred times the medically recommended dosage. In an *American Journal of Psychiatry* study, athletes reported "using as many as five or six steroids simultaneously in cycles lasting from four to twelve weeks." Soon a black market developed to satisfy the ever-increasing demand for "stacking" one steroid type on another.

As awareness of the health risks rose, doctors who had been ambivalent about steroids became strident critics and steered away from prescribing them. This further separated athletes from sound medical advice and physical checkups, and many, hooked on steroids, turned to the underground. What started as a promising experiment had soured. The athletic community learned a medical lesson Peter Latham described best more than a century ago: "Poisons and medicine are oftentimes the same substance given with different intents."

WHAT'S IN THE NAME?

The technical name is *anabolic-androgenic steroids*. That's quite a mouthful, but it conveys a lot of information:

Anabolic means tissue-building. The anabolic effect of steroids produces the increased muscle mass many athletes seek.

Androgenic means masculinizing. The androgenic effect of steroids increases the body's masculinity, often in unwanted side effects such as the voice-deepening or breast-shrinking result that females using steroids experience.

All steroids produce both anabolic and androgenic body changes; they build tissue *and* increase the athlete's masculinity. Drug manufacturers have tried to design steroids that retain the anabolic (tissue-building) effect while minimizing the androgenic (masculinizing) effect; that's one reason the pharmacist's shelves stock several dozen steroid versions. To date, though, no manufacturer has been successful in separating the adverse effects. That's because all manufactured steroids must share the basic chemical structure that we will discuss next.

HOW DO SYNTHETICS PASS FOR TESTOSTERONE?

Natural steroids are formed in microorganisms, vertebrates, and some higher plants. They have been part of life for a billion years.

To pass as an effective copy, *the synthetic steroid must look and act like the body's naturally produced testosterone*; that means that it must have native testosterone's basic chemical structure. If not, your body won't respond to steroids as it does to testosterone.

All manufactured steroids "act" real enough to pass the body's detection system. As the following illustration makes clear, each

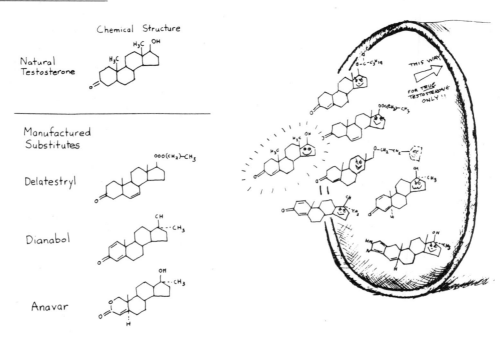

manufactured copy retains testosterone's basic atomic skeleton. The minor variations don't interfere with their designated task: passing for native testosterone.

HOW DO ORAL AND INJECTABLE STEROIDS DIFFER?

When asked what steroids he had trained on, former football pro Lyle Alzado responded, "I did a combination of all of it. It cost me twenty to thirty thousand dollars a year." Alzado died of a brain tumor.

Anabolic steroids are injected or taken orally, depending on the drug's exact design. The oral steroids (pills) are water-soluble; when the athlete discontinues use, the system quickly eliminates traces of the steroids. This creates a problem for authorities who attempt to detect steroid use among athletes.

Injectable steroids can be either water-soluble or fat-soluble. The body's fat cells absorb the fat-soluble steroids, and as the fat cells are depleted for energy, the steroids are slowly released into the bloodstream. Fat-soluble steroids are the most easily detected, since small amounts can remain stored in the fat deposits for many months.

HOW IS THE MUSCLE CELLS' CHEMISTRY AFFECTED?

Once in the bloodstream, testosterone look-alikes diffuse across the cell membrane into the muscle cell, where it binds to a receptor molecule that normally binds only to native testosterone. The receptor molecule can't tell the difference.

When bound together, the steroid and receptor form a complex that enters the muscle cell's nucleus and acts as a biological switch, turning on the cell's genetic machinery (DNA). Once activated, the DNA directs the production of protein through amino acids and other raw materials floating in the cell.

This protein production goes on every day without the steroids. But experts believe that the combined supply of steroids and native testosterone can activate more receptor molecules than native testosterone can alone, resulting in increased protein production. The body then uses the extra protein for more muscle-cell growth than could occur without the steroids.

HOW DO STEROIDS CAUSE UNWANTED SIDE EFFECTS?

Testosterone-sensitive receptor molecules are part of the normal cellular machinery of all body tissue—the brain, skin, blood, bone, and reproductive organs, as well as muscle. Like natural testosterone, anabolic steroids ride the bloodstream and interact with all tissue types by activating their receptor molecules.

The causal connection between steroid use and unwanted side effects follows two paths: Either the athlete consumes too much of the steroid, or the minor variations in certain manufactured steroids' chemical structure are toxic (poisonous) to the athlete's system. In practice, the causes often overlap.

Physical side effects fall into two categories. Some steroids cause unwanted changes by overstimulating receptor cells in a wide range of tissue. For example, activating the skin's testosterone-sensitive receptor cells will increase oiliness and facial-hair growth—steroid-induced changes that females frequently experience. The second category involves the liver, which functions to rid toxins from the body. Certain steroids, because of the slight structural differences separating them from natural testosterone, are toxic. If the athlete consumes steroids in great quantity, the liver's detoxifying machinery is overloaded. The result is a toxic liver, unable to perform its normal vital functions.

In summary, remember that side effects are related to quantity consumed and/or the minor variations in the manufactured steroid's chemical structure.

DOES STEROID USE HAVE PSYCHOLOGICAL EFFECTS?

In *Drugs, Sports and Politics*, Dr. Robert Voy writes that he has seen "mood swings, increased libido, sexual perversion, violent, uncontrollable behavior, and even psychotic episodes among athletes who used anabolic-androgenic steroids."

Of course, those same behaviors are found among athletes who don't use steroids. Certainly research cannot generalize that steroids elicit specific behavioral problems; if that were the case, all steroid users would be affected. Even so, anecdotal reports repeatedly recall "steroid rages"—aggressive outbursts among users.

Is there a biological connection? Recent studies have established testosterone receptors in regions of the central nervous system, including the limbic area, which is associated with aggressive behavior. It is not an unreasonable suggestion that steroids might increase the propensity for aggression by bonding to more receptors.

Unquestionably, hormones affect thoughts and behavior; as hormonal balances change throughout life, so do conduct and emotions. But there is a paucity of research into steroids' psychological effects. Harrison Pope, M.D., and David Katz, M.D., did publish one widely reported study in the *American Journal of Psychiatry*. Through structured retrospective interviews (recall), the study examined forty-one steroid users. Five users were concluded to have experienced transient psychotic episodes, and nine experienced manic or depressive episodes.

On the other hand, thousands of longtime steroid users have shown no adverse psychological effects. Some athletes might use steroids as an excuse for behavioral problems, or steroids might aggravate an already-aggressive personality. The jury is still out.

DO FEMALES RESPOND TO ANABOLIC STEROIDS?

Steroids build the female athlete's muscle. In fact, given equal doses, anabolic steroids produce a more profound tissue-building effect for females than males. But the female also experiences remarkable gender-related side effects—a sometimes irreversible body masculinization.

The flood of testosteronelike steroids throws the female regulatory systems out of balance. Her normal blood level of native testosterone is only one-tenth that of a male; when ingesting steroids, depending on the quantity consumed, her blood level of testosteronelike chemicals can substantially *exceed* the average male's.

Normally, the female athlete's lower level of circulating testosterone makes it less probable that a testosterone molecule will contact a testosterone-sensitive receptor molecule. Hence, most of the testosterone-sensitive receptors in her muscle, skin, genital, and bone tissue remain inactive. Her hormone regulatory system keeps many receptor "switches" turned off.

Even a doctor's advice can be incorrect, as evidenced by the 1970s and 1980s editions of the *Physician's Desk Reference*, which stated: "**WARNING**: ANABOLIC STEROIDS DO NOT ENHANCE ATHLETIC ABILITY."

Injecting steroids overrides the female hormonal system's checks and balances. The large quantity of normally vacant receptors are switched on by the flood of testosterone substitutes. Activating the testosterone receptors starts a chain reaction that produces protein, muscle growth's raw material. Coupled with intense resistance training, the female grows more muscle and becomes stronger than she could have without the steroids. Many female bodybuilders' remarkable musculature is a product of resistance training and testosterone substitutes.

Steroids do more than increase muscle mass and strength. Soviet and Eastern Bloc female throwers were quietly consuming anabolic steroids as long ago as the early 1950s. Later in the decade, steroid use spread from the throwing events to any sport requiring speed and strength. But along with record throws and jumps, female athletes were looking more masculine and suffering health problems.

Steroids consumed for muscle growth and enhanced sports performance are basically the same drugs that prepare a female for a transsexual operation, changing the secondary sex characteristics from woman to man. The steroids overactivate the testosterone-sensitive receptor cells of the skin, bone, and sex organs. With that in mind, you can understand steroids' remarkable effects on the female body, including a deeper voice, increased facial and body hair, baldness, infertility, breast shrinkage, clitoral enlargement, and menstrual irregularities. The preceding list is by no means complete; it points out only the most obvious androgenic effects specific to the female's body. Additionally, the female athlete doesn't escape health risks common to both sexes, including acne, liver dysfunction, immune-system suppression, and steroid-induced psychological problems.

Are female steroid-users at greater risk than males? Because females start with more vacant testosterone receptors, it is more probable that steroids can reach and activate a vacant testosterone-sensitive receptor in female tissue. What is a small steroid quantity for a male will produce a definite masculinizing effect in the female: All women suffer masculinization effects from steroids. But whether the female is at greater risk of side effects common to both sexes is debatable. In either case, the female considering steroid use should remember that the risk is always present.

WHAT ARE THE EFFECTS OF STEROID USE DURING ADOLESCENCE?

Adolescence is when most young men and many young women begin weight training. It's also the first time that many consider steroids to speed muscle growth.

A 1990 federal government report estimated that 262,000 students between seventh and twelfth grade had used anabolic steroids. A *Journal of the American Medical Association* study stated that one-third of adolescent steroid users begin before age fifteen, and another one-third before reaching sixteen.

The physical consequences of adding steroids to the adolescent's developing body are not fully understood, even by the most experienced health-care professionals. Since most athletes purchase steroids illegally, with little advice beyond gym gossip, the risks are compounded.

Adolescent steroid use must be considered on two fronts. First, adolescent users are apparently subject to the same general health risks as adults. Second, an oversupply of testosterone substitutes (steroids) alters the subtle hormonal balance that guides the adolescent's body through the growth process. Is the damage temporary or permanent? Are health risks immediate, long-range, or both?

Steroids reportedly stunt the adolescent's skeletal growth. The excessive testosterone-substitutes activate growth-plate cell receptors that, once activated, initiate growth-plate hardening, preventing further longitudinal growth.

Steroids may also cause long-term sterility problems in the adolescent male. Sensing the testosterone substitutes' presence, the testes shut down native testosterone production, resulting in reduced sperm count. With adult males, the shutdown is temporary; natural production returns to normal several months after steroids are discontinued. Because the adolescent male is in the process of sexual development, however, he might not be as fortunate in reestablishing normal sperm production. Many experts believe that steroids' interference may produce long-term sterility.

The adolescent female manifests steroid-induced responses similar to adult females', plus potential bone closure. Most significant is the masculinization pattern: baldness, subcutaneous fat reduction, and a corresponding loss of "feminine shape."

For males or females, turning to steroids increases the risk of illness—now and in the long term.

HOW DOES STEROID USE AFFECT KIDS?

That the issue surfaces at all might seem preposterous, but pediatricians and coaches are frequently quizzed about steroids and growth hormones by eager fathers who hope to give their son or daughter a competitive edge. They appreciate steroids' ability to enhance performance in sports, but lack an equal understanding of the risks. Steroids do produce significant muscle growth in both boys and girls—perhaps at a greater rate than that for the adult male. But when weighed against the potential side effects, administering steroids to children is absurdly dangerous.

Steroids have been widely distributed in the United States since the early 1960s. In fact, hundreds of thousands of athletes have used steroids without apparent side effects, causing them to ignore the health risks that steroids might present to others. I've heard more than one father tell his young son that "steroids didn't hurt me." Perhaps the young athlete's coach, or a conversation overheard at the gym, gives the same idea. Regardless of motivation, a steroid habit begun in childhood has the potential for enormous destruction. The topic needs to be discussed.

The prepubescent's desire for steroid-induced muscle growth is analogous to the adult female's. The prepubescent has about one-tenth of the adult male's testosterone level. Ingesting testosterone substitutes substantially increases the probability that native testosterone or the testosterone substitute will activate the muscle cells' testosterone-sensitive receptors. Once activated, the receptor complex initiates muscle-building protein production.

The thought of children taking steroids is terrifying, because no one knows the extent of the side effects that might result from even small dosages. There is no question that the testosterone substitutes alter the body's natural timing and development. The boy's body does not naturally increase testosterone production until puberty; the girl's production never increases.

Medical authorities generally agree that steroids add muscle, but the chemicals also prematurely close the child's growth plates, ultimately resulting in shorter adult stature than would have been attained. How much height is lost depends on the quantity of steroids consumed, but as with adult females, small quantities produce dramatic effects.

Other than retarded growth and masculinization of both sexes, is the child at greater risk than the adult user? Most experts presume that kids are at greater risk in both the short and long term. A steroid that works wonders for an adult might produce horrible side effects in a child that won't manifest until later in life. No one knows the extent to which steroids interfere with a young person's complex developmental process.

Giving children steroids is like betting their lives on a dice roll. The only possible gain is premature muscle growth, a size increase that will occur naturally at puberty. In return, growth is stunted, natural development is stymied, and short-term and long-range illnesses may develop.

Part Two

TRAINING SMART

CHAPTER SEVEN

BASIC PRINCIPLES AND STYLES OF STRENGTH TRAINING

Regardless of your age, sex, or sport, a handful of basic principles and training styles are necessary information. Let's look.

TRAINING PRINCIPLE #1. HIGH-TENSION MUSCLE CONTRACTIONS

Strength-training exercises require high-tension contractions.

Muscular strength is the greatest force the muscle can produce during a single contraction (a tension buildup within the muscle). A muscular contraction's tension is much like pulling on the ends of a rubber band. Rather than pulling away from the center to build the tension, though, the muscle tenses by pulling toward its center. In order to build strength, an exercise must produce tension approaching the muscle's maximal limit. Low tension doesn't stimulate an adaptive response.

TRAINING PRINCIPLE #2. HEAVY LOADS

Strength gains come quickest with few repetitions and heavy resistance.

Building strength requires relatively heavy weights. The greater the weight, the more intense the muscle contraction necessary to complete the lift. In practice, the weight determines how many reps you'll do. That's common sense: The heavier an object, the fewer times you can lift it.

Sets, reps, and selecting appropriate weights are extensively covered in the next chapter. For now, we'll just repeat the principle: Heavy weights and low reps are strength training's benchmark.

TRAINING PRINCIPLE #3. OVERLOAD

The strength-training program must overload the muscles.

Your muscles grow stronger or weaker based on the demands placed on them. An *overload* is a greater demand than the muscle normally encounters—the weight is difficult for the muscle to lift, as when an athlete who normally lifts 100 pounds lifts 120 pounds (the overload). Workout after workout, the exercise remains difficult unless your body adapts by physically changing your muscular and nervous systems. The physical changes (see chapter 1) increase your muscle's strength capacity.

A less rigorous training schedule also brings about change. Your body reallocates resources away from the muscle, reducing its strength—it *detrains*. The same thing happens during a layoff. "Use it or lose it" applies here.

Lifting a heavier weight is one way to overload a muscle. Increasing the number of sets, reducing rest periods, and working out more frequently are other methods that the next chapter covers.

TRAINING PRINCIPLE #4. PROGRESSIVE OVERLOADING

As the muscles strengthen, resistance must be continually increased.

Progressive overload training (also called progressive resistance) has a basic premise: When the body adapts to a given stress level, increase the stress to begin new adaptation.

Much like climbing stairs, overloads rise step by step. After negotiating the first, you must move on to the second. Properly done, progressive overload training is a long-term process.

TRAINING PRINCIPLE #5. SPECIFICITY OF MOVEMENT

Duplicate your sport's movements as closely as possible.

You strength-train to improve your athletic ability. That means that your weight-room exercises should duplicate your sport's movements. The closer the match, the more probable that the increased strength will apply. That's the *principle of specificity*.

When unable to precisely duplicate the movement, the next-best choice is to train sport-specific muscles. As an extreme example, a long jumper wouldn't spend most of his time exercising the throwing muscles. Neither would a pitcher primarily exercise to improve his jump. The smart athlete develops the muscles most heavily relied upon in his or her sport.

TYPES OF STRENGTH TRAINING

What kind of equipment and training system is best? Which system and equipment produces peak performance? There is a difference. Following are the various training systems, their equipment needs, and the respective results.

DYNAMIC CONTRACTIONS—WHEN MUSCLES MOVE

During a dynamic contraction, a muscle *changes length*. As tension builds, pulling the muscle's ends toward the center, the muscle shortens or lengthens. Every athletic movement, from simplest to most complex, relies on dynamic contraction. That's because the bones attached to each end of a skeletal muscle must move for the muscle to change length. Except for isometrics, all training systems described in this chapter involve dynamic contraction.

Dynamic contractions are further divided into two categories, depending on whether the contraction occurs when the muscle shortens (concentric contraction) or lengthens (eccentric contraction).

Isotonic Training

Isotonic training and equipment have been strength training's mainstays for three thousand years. In ancient Greece, it was Milo lifting his pet bull. Today, millions hoist barbells and dumbbells.

With isotonic exercise and equipment, the resistance is consistent throughout the movement. A barbell's weight—the resistance to movement—remains the same from the lift's beginning to its end.

Isotonic training has limitations: A barbell that is an optimal overload at one point in the exercise is too little at another. Imagine the variation in difficulty at a barbell curl's different points. The top twenty degrees are easy compared to the moment at which the barbell is held at a right angle to the body. The training implication is that one angle receives the desired training effect, while all other joint angles are underworked.

Variable-Resistance Training

Variable-resistance training came into vogue with the spread of

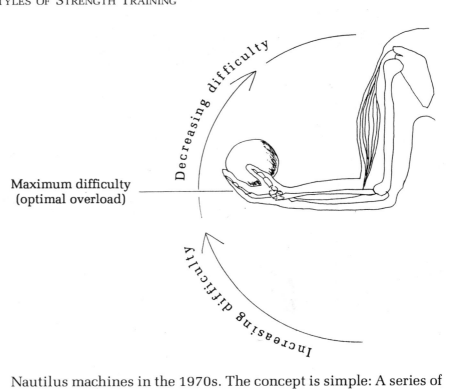

Maximum difficulty
(optimal overload)

Nautilus machines in the 1970s. The concept is simple: A series of mechanical devices, called cams or sleeves, modulate the machine's effective resistance (weight) to match the muscle's capacity at different points of the exercise.

Imagine a barbell curl during which the resistance is continually changed to match the bicep's capacity at each angle. That's the concept of variable-resistance machines. The resistance changes in concert with the joint angle, so that the muscle is overloaded throughout the range of movement. Unlike isotonic training, there are no easy joint angles.

Variable resistance training equipment seems superior to barbells and dumbbells; anything that polished and expensive should do a better job. But research doesn't back intuition in this case. Variable-resistance equipment has proven to be as good as free weights for building strength, but not better.

Speed Loading

Speed loading's object is to perform a movement as fast as possible. Both variable-resistance and isotonic equipment can be used.

Speed-loading exercises can be valuable, especially when training for power. Refer back to chapter 1, where power is defined as strength multiplied by speed.

As with plyometrics (which will be explained shortly), speed loading generates forces that are too much for beginners or athletes returning from layoffs. In a weight room, injuries highly correlate to sudden movement. Younger athletes, in particular, should refrain from speed loading until they've conditioned the muscles through one year of moderate-speed isotonic training.

Isokinetic Training

Isokinetic training produces a muscle contraction of optimal tension throughout the exercise. In other words, the muscle is optimally stressed as it shortens or lengthens. The practical result is that the strength-training effect accrues to every joint angle.

Isokinetic devices took center stage in the 1970s with the Cybex dynamometer, which the medical and sports community uses for rehabilitation, strength training, and strength testing. Special isokinetic machines vary the resistance throughout the exercise motion, but maintain a constant speed, making them different from resistance equipment.

There is some evidence that the training velocity at which the machine is set is important to sports application. Studies suggest that strength is increased only at or below training velocity. If this is true, an athlete would want to preset the machine to approximate that of his or her sport.

The theory of isokinetic training assumes that an athlete will expend maximal effort throughout the movement; the machine pushes back only as hard as you push. If you have access to isokinetic devices, use them.

Plyometric Training

Plyometric exercises stretch, or "preload," a muscle before it shortens through contraction. The stretch stores elastic energy—much like a rubber band—which is released during the muscle contraction.

Here's an example: An athlete drops from a standing position atop a box to a squatting position on the floor—stretching the thigh muscle on landing. Without pause, he intensely contracts the thighs, jumping as high as possible. This particular drop/stretch/contract sequence develops explosive leg power. In fact, plyometric exercises have proven to increase jumping height more than two inches in as little as eight weeks. The load (the resistance the muscle must overcome) would be increased by using a higher box or wearing a weighted vest. Plyometrics are most often used for leg training, but the concept adapts to any body part.

Plyometrics' downside is increased injury risk from the violent landings and takeoffs; the stretch-contraction produces greater force than do standard weight training movements. For this reason, approach plyometrics with caution; start with a low box and add height after the muscle adequately adapts to the drop-jump stress. Beginning strength trainers, or those returning from a layoff, should not include plyometrics until the appropriate muscle groups are prepared with less violent exercises.

The key concept is that plyometrics stretch the muscle before it contracts. The elastic energy stored during the stretch combines with the usual contractile machinery, making a super-contraction.

Isometric Training

Isometric training is pushing or pulling against an immovable object. Nothing moves when you push against a wall, but push hard enough and you'll feel your contracting muscles stress. During an isometric exercise, the contracting muscle is intentionally prevented from moving the attached bones. The muscle *can't* change length because the immovable object won't permit it, even at maximal tension. Place one hand under your desk and try to curl; that's an isometric contraction. The technical name is *static contraction.*

Static contractions are important in many sports. For example, every time you hold a weight motionless, your muscles undergo static contractions. Still, isometric's sports applications are limited because they build strength only at the specific angle being exercised. This also holds true for muscular endurance. If the elbow is bent at 90 degrees during the isometric exercise, the increased strength applies only when the elbow is at that angle.

The vast majority of athletic activities require strength application through a partial or full range of joint movement. For this reason, isometric exercise won't satisfy athletes' dynamic strength needs.

Isometric exercises are important to an overall strength-training program, however, and are a good way to get past sticking points in an isotonic movement. For example, if the sticking point is midway through a curl, several weeks of isometric curls at that angle will improve strength at that point.

Sports also have integral isometric components. Archery provides a perfect example. Imagine the muscles of the wrist, shoulder and arm isometrically contracting as the archer steadies the bow string in the pulled position. Isometric training in this position will enhance stability during the hold.

Keep an open mind about isometrics, and you'll find applications for your sport-training program.

Choosing Equipment

Free weights or machines? The expensive Nautilus, Cybex, and Universal equipment rely on the same strength-training principles as a set of garage-sale barbells. Your choice should depend on safety, economics, and convenience.

A set of the more popular machines costs between $25,000 and $150,000. A barbell set that exercises the same muscles costs between $100 and $1,000. An "all-in-one" weight-training machine costs several hundred dollars.

Machines do have advantages. They are safer when properly used by an athlete who fits the machine. Weight selection is more convenient, and saves time in high-use weight rooms. But free weights allow more natural body motions, and can be used safely regardless of your body's size.

Are machines better at building strength? No. Studies have found that the training system, not the equipment, determines how fast you gain strength.

The optimal weight-training room has a variety of equipment, but you can gain strength lifting bricks, bulls, or your own body weight. Equipment is one of your program's least important elements.

CHAPTER EIGHT

SETS, REPS, WEIGHT, REST, AND SEASONAL VARIATIONS

How many sets and reps are best? How many training days? How much weight should I use? What's the difference between an in-season and off-season schedule? These are frequent questions, but there is no perfect set, rep, weight, and rest composite. The right balance for one athlete might injure another.

Research has proven that any program of one to ten sets and one to ten reps increases strength. Skeletal maturity, physical condition, psychological stamina, hormone balance, time available, and the season are some factors that influence the weights, sets, reps, and rest you select. The key is finding what works for you.

The following recommendations are based on programs that have worked successfully for athletes of various sports. First, you'll select the right weight.

HOW MUCH WEIGHT SHOULD I USE?

Strength-training research is conclusive: *Nothing matters more than choosing the correct weight.* This produces maximum muscle tension on the set's last rep, allowing not even one more rep than planned.

Trial and error is one way to find the correct weight for any number of reps. Another way depends on knowing the maximum weight you can lift for one repetition of the exercise movement—the one-rep maximum (abbreviated 1RM). For example, if you can bench-press 300 pounds *one time only*, 300 pounds is your 1RM for the bench press. Once you know that, selecting the correct weight for any number of reps is a simple calculation.

The procedure for determining a 1RM depends on age, experience, and training condition. Use the following guidelines:

Finding Your 1RM

1. Experienced adult and late-teen athletes: Use a trial-and-error method one rep at a time, adding plates until the weight cannot be lifted. The last successfully lifted weight is the 1RM.

If the athlete is new to weight training, the supervisor should *conservatively* estimate the 1RM. A more accurate assessment can wait until the athlete has acquired correct form, particularly with exercises involving overhead lifts or substantial, unsupported, lower-back stress.

2. Prepubescent and midgrowth-spurt athletes: 1RMs should be estimated by an experienced coach, because prepubescents must not perform maximum lifts. The 1RM can be infrequently assessed by trial and error with qualified supervision, but only with exercises in which the body is safely supported.

HOW DOES THE 1RM DETERMINE THE HIGHER-REPS WEIGHT?

Knowing your 1RM makes weight selection easy. The following chart, constructed after the work of M.J.N. McDonagh and C.T.M. Davies, presents the weight-rep combination as a percentage of the 1RM.

Now you can match the reps and weight. If the training schedule calls for three sets of six reps for the bench press, and your 1RM is 200 pounds, the correct weight for your set is 156 pounds. Using the chart, a six-rep set calls for a weight 78 percent of the 1RM.

FIGURE 8-1

Reps	% of 1 RM	Hypothetical poundage for a lifter with a 1 RM of 315
1	100%	315 lbs.
2	95%	299 lbs.
3	86%	271 lbs.
4	78%	246 lbs.
5	70%	221 lbs.
6	61%	192 lbs.
7	53%	167 lbs.

HOW MANY SETS AND REPS ARE RECOMMENDED?

As noted before, research substantiates that any reasonable set/rep combination will improve strength. The following recommendations compile patterns that have worked consistently:

Late-teen and adult athletes

Sports Strength Program exercises: three sets of six repetitions. This is the *most efficient* rep/set pattern for the experienced athlete, when factoring the investment against the return, but it will not build strength *faster*. In fact, five sets of six reps build strength more quickly than three sets of six. The following chart illustrates the point at which sets increase, the relative returns diminish.

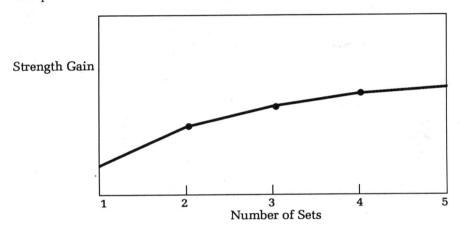

Supplementary exercises: three sets of ten repetitions.

The supplementary exercises augment strength developed through the Sports Strength Program. Those in this book are sport-specific. The difference in rep counts ensures that emotional and physical intensity is maintained during the Sports Strength Program.

Early-adolescent athletes

Sports Strength Program exercises: two sets of ten repetitions.
   Supplementary exercises: two sets of twelve reps.

Prepubescent athletes

Sports Strength Program exercises: two sets of ten repetitions.
   Supplementary exercises: two sets of twelve reps.

Beginners (or athletes returning from layoffs): All ages

Sports Strength Program exercises: two sets of twelve repetitions for one month.

Supplementary exercises: one set of twelve repetitions for one month.

Safety and conditioning demand that beginners and athletes returning from a layoff use twelve-repetition sets for the first month. Follow your age group's recommendations after that.

ARE THERE OPTIONAL PATTERNS FOR EXPERIENCED ATHLETES?

If you're an experienced late-teen or adult strength-athlete, you can experiment with set/rep combinations. Begin by trying those that have worked for other athletes, if only for variety. Here are some:

Multiple-set system

Multiple-set system is a catch-all phrase for various set/rep combinations. It usually combines two or three warm-up sets followed by three to six more intense sets at a constant resistance.

Most authors quote Richard Berger, whose *Research Quarterly* (1963) recommended three intense sets of six repetitions for "optimal" strength development. However, later research suggests that the more sets you execute, the faster strength improves. The absolute strength return per set slows with each additional set beyond the first, though, so you have to decide where to draw the line. Refer back to the chart that illustrates how relative returns diminish as sets increase.

Multiple sets can be manipulated to safely meet any training parameters. The prepubescent can perform single sets of ten or twelve repetitions and gain strength. The experienced adult can increase training intensity with six sets of six to eight reps. All others can find a niche somewhere in between.

There are drawbacks to multiple-set systems. Most athletes approach strength training as a tool, not an end in itself, so multiple sets often reduce the desire to train.

Feed on multiple-set systems, but not as a steady diet. Incorporate other set/rep systems in your training program for variety, and for the broadest range of adaptational response.

Pyramid systems

The pyramid system has been popular for the past fifty years, and it can follow two paths. A light-to-heavy pyramid begins with a light-weight set (10RM), and increases weight with each successive set. The rep count drops with each succeeding set until the final single-rep set with a maximum lift (1RM). The heavy-to-light pyramid starts with a heavy single-rep first set (1RM), followed by sets of successively lighter weights and higher reps. For variety, alternate between the two. If you have the time and energy, try a double pyramid, light/heavy/light or heavy/light/heavy.

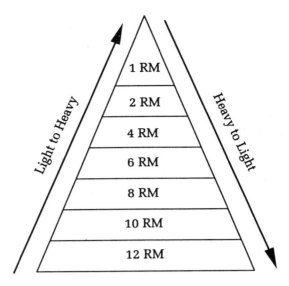

Athletes from all sports have used pyramids to build significant strength, and research confirms their practical experience. Physiologically, the varied set/rep sequence activates all possible motor units.

Pyramids are not for the physically immature or beginners, because the heavier sets are close to or at maximal capacity. But experienced adults and late adolescents should get good results.

Single-set-to-failure

Matt Brzycki, strength and fitness coordinator at Princeton University, states the case for a single set to muscular failure: "A high-intensity (or single-set) program can be just as productive as a multiple-set program, provided each set is performed to the point of absolute muscular failure. Whereas a multiple-set program is successful due to the cumulative effect of each *set*, a single-set-to-failure is successful due to the cumulative effect of each *repetition*."

The key to success: The set ends at the absolute last possible rep. Don't stop before failure. At failure with the original weight, some coaches remove plates to allow several more reps, or a training partner can assist as needed. The extra reps' added intensity is thought to build strength.

Researchers give the system mixed reviews. A single-set-to-failure significantly increases strength, but most studies indicate that traditional multiple-set systems produce greater gains for more people.

There are situations when a single-set-to-failure makes the most sense. When training time is limited, single sets might be necessary, whether for an entire playing season, or in a temporary situation. The single-set-to-failure is also circuit training's mainstay, the combination equipment manufacturers push to increase traffic-flow through commercial gyms.

Inject the single-set-to-failure into the workout day when you need an extra boost.

Forced reps to failure

Forced reps, also called assisted reps, are performed with a training partner who helps only enough for the lifter to complete the movement. Theoretically, and from my personal experience, *sets of forced reps produce the most rapid gains*. That's a big statement, so let's describe the steps:

1. The athlete selects a weight that he or she expects to lift for two unassisted reps (2RM).
2. At failure with the selected weight, the athlete continues the exercise movement with the spotter's assistance, who aids no more than absolutely necessary, perhaps to pass a sticking point.
3. The set is complete when the lifter reaches practical exhaustion (ten to twelve reps)—about 25 percent of the initial force.
4. The procedure is repeated for a second set.

The success comes from each set's intensity. Forced reps provide the training effect manufacturers of isokinetic and variable-resistance exercise devices seek, because the spotter assists only where and as much as necessary. The athlete functions at *maximal capacity* during each repetition, unable to push or pull any harder. With traditional unassisted reps, the athlete operates at near-maximal capacity only during the last one or two repetitions.

High-intensity, forced-rep sets aren't for the beginner, the pre-pubescent, or pre–growth spurt adolescent athletes. They are analogous to a series of maximal lifts, which younger, inexperienced athletes must avoid.

Negative rep sets

People generally envision a muscle shortening as tension builds—a concentric contraction. A practical example is the muscle-shortening contraction that pulls the hand toward the shoulder when you curl a barbell. Negative reps, however, emphasize eccentric contractions, during which the muscle lengthens. A practical example occurs as the biceps resists the barbell's motion during the curl's downward phase (see Figure 7-1).

Theoretically, exercises causing the greatest muscle tension bring the greatest strength gains. Negative reps produce the most muscular tension of any repetition system by using heavier weights during the exercise's muscle-lengthening phase than can be lifted during the muscle-shortening phase. An athlete able to curl 100 pounds for ten reps would use 120 pounds for ten reps of negative curls. Sets and reps remain the same.

Research indicates that negative reps build at least as much strength as any other system. But because few studies have been done, it cannot be conclusively stated that negative reps are best.

Negative reps do have drawbacks. First, the greater muscle tension increases delayed muscle soreness, necessitating longer rest intervals and fewer workouts. Second, negative reps often require a spotter. How else could you accomplish a superheavy set of negative bench presses?

Negative reps offer variety for experienced adults, but practical wisdom suggests that beginners, prepubescents, and adolescents who have not finished the growth spurt should avoid this system, as they would any maximal lifts.

HOW MUCH REST BETWEEN SETS?

Rest two to three minutes between sets. The rest period is essentially the same for all strength trainers. The length is a function of how the body energizes muscle. Strength training, because of the set's short duration, relies on the muscle's internal energy source. You can't wait for energy to arrive from outside the muscle cell. Once the muscle's on-hand energy is exhausted, two to three minutes is needed for the energy store to rebuild for the next set; otherwise, the muscles cannot fully respond to the training demands.

Energy reserves gradually diminish if the same muscle group is worked for several exercises. This requires longer rest periods as the workout progresses. Working another group in between, however, will get the rest periods back on schedule. High-intensity, forced-rep-to-failure sets will obviously require more rest.

One last comment: At times, mental determination lags behind physical ability. If that happens, disregard the clock. Wait until you are mentally ready to produce a maximum-intensity set.

HOW MUCH REST BETWEEN WORKOUTS?

Rest between workouts depends on the intensity, exercise selection, and the athlete's physical condition, growth stage, and personal experience.

The general guideline is that the body needs time for complete recovery, but not enough to diminish the training effect. The following suggestions are the most commonly recommended:

Caution dictates that prepubescents and rapidly growing early adolescents should wait two days between workouts, until the effect of training can be fully evaluated. Having worked with thousands of strength-trained athletes, I find that this schedule accelerates the adolescent and prepubescent athlete's strength gains, perhaps because the less frequent workouts contribute to greater intensity at the gym. The young athlete can experiment with fewer rest days after demonstrating the capacity to recuperate physically and mentally.

Research, though far from conclusive, suggests that one rest day between workouts is best for most late-teen or adult athletes. An experienced trainer might consider experimenting with more radical patterns, such as two days on and two days off. It is worth noting that elite Olympic weight lifters train as often as five to seven times a week. But beginners, early adolescents, and prepubescents should stay with the mainstream recommendations. Too much work and too little rest early in the program can injure a body.

WHAT ABOUT SEASONAL ADJUSTMENTS?

Building muscle is only one goal. The athlete has to balance the demands of the strength-training schedule with those of his or her sport.

For most athletes, strength workouts are adjusted seasonally. Compared to the off-season workouts, the preseason and competitive season strength workouts are substantially reduced, as more energy and time are allocated to the sport itself. Athletes frequently reduce the number of sets per exercise, the training days per week, or the number of exercises per workout. Whenever you or your coach decide to reduce strength training, consider the following suggestions:

1. Reduce the Sports Strength Program's *sets*, but retain all of its exercises.
2. Reduce the number of workouts per week.
3. Reduce or eliminate non–Sports Strength Program exercises.

Many factors determine what is best for you. You and your coach must balance strength training's importance with competition's time and energy demands.

WHAT IS PERIODIZATION?

Periodization, also called cycling, is a training program lasting for a predetermined number of weeks or months. Each period is divided into five phases of equal length, and each phase has a different pattern of sets, reps, and weights. After passing through each of the five phases, a new cycle is begun.

The following chart offers an example of a training cycle's five distinct phases. Each phase has been arbitrarily set at four weeks. School scheduling, preseason training time, and personal choice determine a phase's appropriate length.

Variation is the essence of periodization. The different set/rep patterns constantly change the stimulus for adaptation. Studies indicate that athletes using periodization programs show significantly greater progress than those using more traditional approaches.

Periodization Model Chart

Phase	Hypertrophy	Basic Strength Development	Strength and Power Building	Peaking for Event	Active Rest
Sets	3–8	3–5	3–5	1–3	Physical play: handball, cross-training, etc.
Reps	8–12	4–6	2–3	1–3	
Days/week	3–4	3–5	3–5	1–5	

When using the Periodization chart, determine the correct weight of reps by referring to the chart by McDonagh and Davies on the bottom of page 73.

CHAPTER NINE

TRAINING SAFELY

"Every time a man pitches, he is systematically injuring his arm. A pitcher's durability will depend on the genetic capacity of the arm to recover from the insult of pitching."

—Dr. James C. Parkes II, New York Mets team physician, in *The New York Times Magazine*, June 15, 1980

Injuries are a fact of life for most athletes, but a few common-sense precautions can prevent many injuries, making training and competing safer.

SUPERVISION

When you don't know how to do something, it makes sense to ask for advice. An experienced trainer can offer lots of helpful tips on preventing injuries.

Supervision is particularly valuable when performing an exercise for the first time. Sure, a book can describe a weight-room exercise, and most gyms are lined with mirrors for personal feedback, but nothing replaces a competent coach's objectivity. He or she can spot potential problems before they lead to harm, as well as shed light on nutrition, equipment, clothing, sets, reps, and loads. Why take any aspect of strength training for granted?

EMPHASIZE PREPUBESCENT AND ADOLESCENT SUPERVISION

All professional organizations that endorse strength training for younger athletes insist on adult supervision. Adults are not always smarter than adolescents, but their advice and warnings come from experience.

As a result, a supervisor can channel youthful exuberance into realistic expectations, connecting moderate workouts to a long-range plan. They'll guard against overtraining and the lure of lifting too-heavy weights.

Most of all, the supervisor is responsible for explaining the rationale behind the rules, so that the athlete can apply the knowledge to other situations. Effective supervision is educational.

SPOTTERS

Always use a spotter (or spotters) when performing overhead lifts or supporting a weight above your waist, and have a spotter stand by through all the sets, not just when completing the last few reps. "Better safe than sorry" makes sense: You're the one who will be stuck under a barbell if you misjudge your strength.

Spotters are particularly important when recovering from an injury. Even with the lightest sets, the injury might flare up anew. In that case, the spotter should immediately remove the resistance. Don't attempt to finish the lift alone.

Finally, make sure your spotter is skilled and strong enough to get you out of trouble. By the time someone rushes across the gym to assist, you may be already hurt.

EQUIPMENT CONCERNS

Both coaches and athletes want the safest equipment, but there is no one best piece or manufacturer for all people. To varying degrees, it depends on who will use the equipment.

Weight-training machines don't fit all bodies; most kids and very small or very large adults fall outside their safe size range. That's the case whether the manufacturer is Nautilus, Cybex, Universal, Soloflex, Weider, or any other brand. Short arms may be unable to replace a barbell on a bench-press support safely; short legs might be unable to replace the weight atop a squat machine.

Another danger concerns the rotation axis of machines that operate off a cam. A too-small or too-large body can't conform to the cam-controlled orbit while correctly gripping the bar. Pullover machines cause many shoulder injuries, not because of faulty design, but because the machines don't fit all bodies.

IF THE MACHINE DOESN'T FIT, USE FREE WEIGHTS

Free weights offer an inherent safety advantage: If a particular machine doesn't fit your body, you can usually duplicate the exercise with a barbell or dumbbell.

Dumbbells are best at permitting natural motion during most upper-body strength-training exercises. The range of motion is often greater than when using either barbells or machines, and dumbbells allow more coordinated movement, bringing added supporting muscles—those assisting the primary movers—into the exercise. Strengthening supporting muscles increases overall joint stability and prepares more muscles for athletic stress. Work dumbbells into your workout.

DON'T NEGLECT COLLARS

Every barbell and dumbbell set comes equipped with collars, but they often sit unused after being removed from the box. Collars can prevent many accidents. The extra seconds that it takes to place a collar on a bar can save torn muscles, broken toes, and bloody brows. Use them, and insist that others do too.

PROPER TECHNIQUE IS A SAFETY PRECAUTION

Practicing proven technique reduces the injury risk. The right way is the safe way.

Two indicators of poor technique, *jerks* and *bounces*, find their way into numerous exercises. Any time a weight is quickly accelerated with a jolt, the muscle and connective tissue experience multiplied force, greatly increasing the chance that they will fail. Let's look at an example:

Does the athlete jerk the barbell off the floor during a clean? Correct technique requires a slow start, as if deadlifting the weight. Once moving, the barbell's velocity should be continually increased throughout the pull. Even with a relatively light weight, a jerk at the beginning heightens the probability of back and shoulder injuries.

Snapping the weight to arm's length can also cause injuries, as can decelerating (stopping) a weight too quickly. Instead, gradually slow it by bending the knees. Proper technique is still the most effective means of injury prevention.

SHOES MATTER TOO

Shoes—the support base for every standing lift—are taken for granted more than any other piece of equipment. Safely executing a strength-training program's various exercises requires a shoe that can withstand forward, backward, and lateral movements. Wear shoes that offer traction, stability, and support when thousands of pounds of force push against them in all directions. Many popular shoes are unable to meet these diverse requirements; most running shoes, for example, are designed for forward motion, not back and side-to-side thrusts.

A safe shoe for weight training is a basketball shoe. That's because a basketball player and a weight lifter each requires a shoe with traction, stability, and shock absorption, while supporting its wearer through a broad range of directional movements. The flat sole spreads the exercise force and prevents rolling during lateral motion.

Once you have selected the proper shoes, use them exclusively for weight training. Don't wreck the traction or smear the soles with oil by wearing them as casual shoes—just one slip with a heavy weight on your shoulders could result in disaster.

WARM UP FOR A SAFE WORKOUT!

The objective of a warm-up—preliminary exercise that prepares the body for intense physical stress—is to reduce injury risk. It raises body temperature, because a portion of the chemical reactions energizing the movements is released as heat. The muscle's metabolism rate increases, resulting in faster contraction speed. Preliminary movement increases blood flow (cardiac output) and dilates muscle-tissue capillaries, improving the body's capacity to deliver oxygen to the muscle when more intense exercise begins. Warm-ups also stretch the muscles and connective tissue, making the operative joints more flexible and allowing the athlete to safely perform more intense exercises through a full range of motion.

An effective warm-up includes exercises that increase blood flow while preparing the muscle groups that the workout will focus on. In practice, that means a series of general stretches, followed by five minutes of low-intensity aerobic work elevating cardiac output, and finishing with low-weight, high-rep sets that duplicate the intense exercise movements planned for the training session.

OVERTRAINING LEADS TO INJURIES

"You're not old until it takes you longer to rest up than it does to get tired."

—Dr. Phog Allen, former Kansas basketball coach,
at age seventy-nine

Overtraining is stress that causes a drop in the athlete's performance. Strength training will fatigue muscles, but they will recover with adequate rest; that's a training schedule's normal ebb and flow. If your muscles don't recover before the next workout, you're overtraining.

Last straw

When overtraining leads to injury, small stresses have amassed and finally reached a breaking point. Distance runners experience foot and shin fractures from pounding the pavement each day. Strength athletes experience most overtraining symptoms in muscles and connective tissue, manifesting as continual soreness or even tears.

The more highly motivated the athlete, the more likely he or she will overtrain. Often, the coach must put on the brakes, insisting on adequate recovery time for the workout's stress level. More is not always better.

One way to safeguard against overtraining is to alternate light and heavy training days. Another is to practice major lifts like deadlifts and squats no more than twice a week. Cycling or periodization (see chapter 8) is also effective.

Overtraining's physiological basis is not well understood, but the symptoms are obvious—performance drops. In the past, track coaches recognized the syndrome and called it "staleness." Runners were recording slower times as the season progressed, although training demands remained the same.

Each athlete has a different tolerance. The quest is to find the training loads and rest periods best suited to you. That means drawing the line at which maximal training stress becomes too much stress. In short, experiment. Balance stress and recovery, or you'll reduce performance while increasing the injury potential.

DON'T PUSH TOO HARD AFTER A LAYOFF

After a layoff, don't expect to resume where you left off; muscle responds to the lack of strength training by growing weaker—it detrains.

Detraining is a real physical change. Muscle cells become smaller and are unable to support the pre-layoff training loads. The bones, nervous system, and connective tissue also lose strength. In essence, you're starting to train all over again.

Spend the first post-layoff month training with higher reps (ten) and fewer sets (two) of each exercise. Afterward, reduce the reps and up the sets unless your age category says otherwise.

Is it a waste of time to proceed cautiously? No. You'll protect yourself against extreme soreness—or much worse. Furthermore, if you've recovered from an injury, you need to take particular care when you resume strength training.

COMMON SYMPTOMS AND TREATMENT

Statistically, you are less likely to get hurt when strength-training than when training or participating in many other common physical activities. More injuries occur on the playground's monkey bars, on a football field, or during a pickup basketball game.

But if you do injure yourself during strength training, remember that symptoms and injuries are two different things. A symptom—usually pain—indicates a particular injury, but it isn't a sure diagnosis so much as a signal that something is wrong.

PAIN IS A WARNING TO STOP

Pain is commonly described as sharp, sudden, aching, throbbing, or burning. These subtly different sensory impressions are useful in establishing what is wrong with the body.

When pain occurs also helps to establish the injury's nature and extent. An extreme, sharp pain while performing an exercise is a different indicator than muscular soreness a day or two after an intense workout.

Try to define the different pain signals. Muscle soreness is part of strength training; sharp pain requires immediate attention. Pain is a signal that you should modify your training program; its degree, type, and location determine by how much.

DELAYED ONSET MUSCLE SORENESS (DOMS)

Delayed onset muscle soreness is the muscular pain that athletes experience a day or two after an unusually intense training session. DOMS can be extremely painful, but it's not usually serious.

The pain's physiological basis is damaged muscle cells. The cell membrane is torn, allowing enzymes, nutrients, and contractile proteins to leak out. White blood cells move through the torn membrane into the muscle cell. How many cells are damaged, and how much, determine the degree of pain.

DOMS results from subjecting the muscle to an unaccustomed load. That might require only a light load for an unconditioned athlete, and a very heavy load for an in-shape athlete.

AVOIDING DOMS

Some misinformed strength athletes feel that a workout without soreness is a waste; it's a variation of the "no pain, no gain" mentality. But extreme DOMS disrupts workouts, limiting the rate of strength gains. For that reason alone, serious athletes should not become overly sore.

The best advice is to gradually increase training intensity through a series of workouts; don't try sudden jumps in poundages or set/rep patterns. Allow the muscles to gradually adapt to increased training demands, and don't shock the muscles into injury. That's particularly important advice for beginners, or experienced athletes returning from a seasonal or temporary layoff. Eccentric (muscle-lengthening) contractions produce soreness more often than concentric (muscle-shortening) contractions, so include exercises emphasizing eccentric movements *infrequently*, and perform only one or two sets.

Overload the muscle enough to ensure adaptation, but not enough to produce extreme soreness.

RESUMING TRAINING AFTER DOMS

Strength-training experts hotly debate the best and safest point at which to resume training after DOMS. One group insists that soreness should be completely absent before training the affected muscle groups again. A second group suggests that the pain's degree guide the athlete. If it hurts to exercise with a very light resistance, wait another day or two, until the exercise can be performed pain-free. A third group of authorities suggests that light-weight reps will speed recovery, even when pain is present. The rationale is that exercise increases circulation to the damaged tissue, thereby increasing the healing rate.

My advice: Stretching and light exercise are okay, but don't overstress a damaged muscle. Evaluate the pain; it's the best indicator that you haven't completely recovered from damage. And as long as pain is present, don't overload your muscles.

WHAT ABOUT SERIOUS INJURIES?

Serious weight-room injuries are rare. Anything worse than DOMS usually results from faulty technique, unreasonable overloads, or a lack of attention. But they can occur.

Strains, sprains, and tears vary. It usually takes a medical professional to accurately diagnosis the injury and suggest treatment. If you even suspect a serious injury, immediately seek professional advice. Don't treat the injury yourself.

SHARP PAIN MEANS STOP!

Sharp pain followed by a burning sensation often signals serious injury. Stop training and have it checked.

Not every ache signals a severe problem; some pains result from transient conditions. But if the pain is extreme, continuous, or is accompanied by a burning sensation, stop training until a medical professional examines the source.

TREAT SHARP PAIN WITH RICE

The acronym RICE stands for "rest, ice, compression, elevation"— the treatment sequence recommended for most sports-related injuries. The rationale is that RICE limits swelling. The greater the

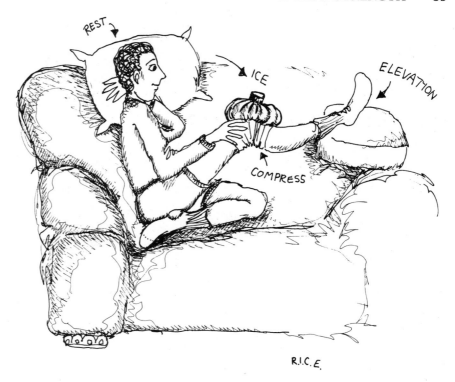

R.I.C.E.

swelling accompanying an injury, the greater the pain and the longer the recovery period, so it makes sense to limit swelling at the outset.

Let's move through the RICE sequence to see how it applies to minor and more serious injuries.

Rest immediately

Rest the injured area; apply no further stress at the first sign of injury.

Ice the injured area immediately

Apply an ice pack to the injured area. Alternate fifteen minutes on and ten minutes off for two hours. Ice helps reduce swelling, decreasing pain.

Compress the injured area

Wrap an elastic bandage around the injured area. The compression helps prevent swelling. Take care to overlap the bandage as you wrap; if it's applied too tightly it might cut circulation.

Elevate the injury

As with ice and compression, elevation's purpose is to impede swelling. Though elevating the torso is impossible, you can prop limbs up higher than the next proximal joint.

GO SLOW AFTER AN INJURY

"I think that's the thing I'm most proud of, coming back from the adversity of those injuries. I never played as well as I would have liked to have played, but I played for thirteen seasons when my doctor thought I would play for four. And I played despite a lot of adversity."

—Joe Namath, pro football player, in *The New York Times*, January 25, 1978

If you are coming back from an injury layoff, pay attention to the workout's pace and intensity. Famous and not-so-famous athletes have ended their competitive careers by returning too quickly to training.

You, your coach, your trainer, and even your doctor can't see everything that's happening below the skin's surface. Rely on physical sensations to guide you back to an appropriate training schedule. Proceed cautiously.

After an injury, resume training with light weights even if you feel perfectly fine. If you reaggravate an injury, you'll lose far more training time than the weeks required to carefully readapt your muscles.

Walk into the weight room with safety first and foremost in mind. Use common sense when selecting equipment and exercises. Always check equipment, and always use collars. Get enough rest, don't overtrain, and eat to maintain and build your body. All these elements help you to avoid injury.

As an athlete, you place intense demands on your body. Sometimes those demands are too great and result in injury. If you do injure yourself while strength-training, don't treat it lightly. Respond to any pain by immediately stopping training. Seek medical attention. It's better to be safe than sorry.

That's enough talk. Now it's time for action—the Sports Strength Program.

Part Three

DESIGNING YOUR WORKOUT

CHAPTER TEN

THE SPORTS STRENGTH PROGRAM: Strengthening the Athlete's Five Basic Movements

Your body's 206 bones and 400 skeletal muscles combine for millions of subtly different athletic movements, and strengthening those muscles and bones improves your capacity to move. But even if you're the most dedicated athlete in the weight room, you don't have the time or equipment to strengthen every specific motion your sport involves. What's the solution?

The Sports Strength Program provides the answer by consolidating those motions into five basic movements—leg and hip thrust, jackknife, back extension, upper-body thrust, and upper-body pull—requiring only five strength exercises that use common weight-room equipment.

The five basic movements and five corresponding strength exercises mimic your body's generalized motions of pushing, pulling, and bending encountered during an athletic event. Strengthening those five movements provides a strong superstructure around which specific athletic motions are built.

For example, imagine a pole vaulter's movements and strength requirements as he thrusts through the takeoff, pulls on the pole, jackknifes the torso upward, and violently extends his back as the

THE FIVE BASIC STRENGTH-BUILDING MOVEMENTS APPLIED TO THE POLE VAULT

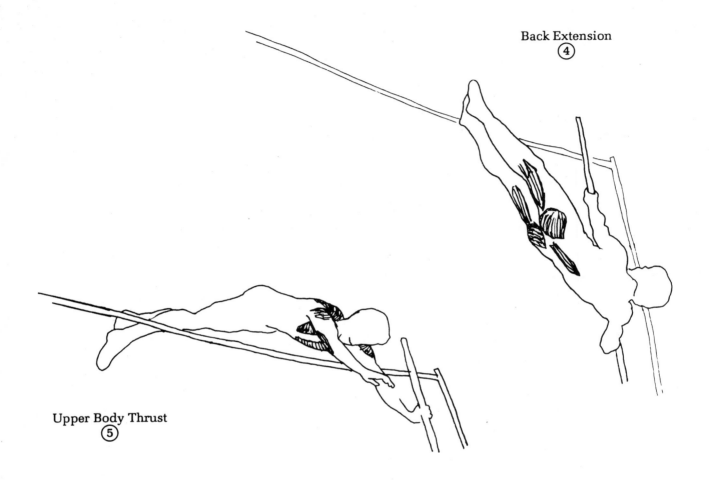

Back Extension
④

Upper Body Thrust
⑤

upper body's thrust propels him over the bar. A weak link at any point means failure.

The Sports Strength Program prevents weak links, strengthening the major muscles responsible for each of the vaulter's basic movements, as well as strengthening the muscles responsible for those of all other athletic events.

Though later you may want to expand your workout by following one of the sport-specific programs found in chapter 13, be assured that the five exercises of your personalized Sports Strength Program alone can fulfill all your basic strength-training requirements.

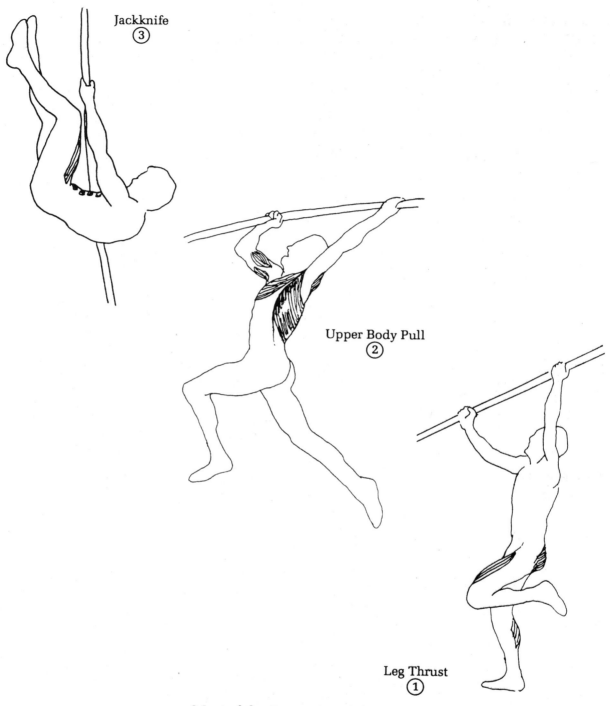

Jackknife
③

Upper Body Pull
②

Leg Thrust
①

Most of the Sports Strength Program's basic movement exercises are *multijoint*, that is, they involve several joints at once.

Consider the leg lunge, a multijoint exercise that strengthens the muscles responsible for hip and leg thrust. One set of leg lunges exercises the same muscle groups as combining one set each of leg curls, leg extensions, calf raises, hip extensions, hip *adductions*,

ROTATIONAL STRENGTH

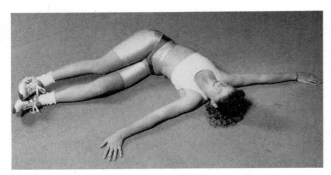

The reverse trunk twist is a basic exercise that strengthens the muscles responsible for torso rotation. See page 140 for correct technique.

Hitting a baseball, putting the shot, and throwing a discus, football, or punch are among many motions that rely on the torso's rotational strength.

Although not listed as a basic movement, rotational-strength exercises are indispensable for athletes who depend on torso rotation. Unfortunately, people frequently neglect these muscles, assuming that rotation begins with leg drive and ends at the hips. It's true, for example, that the discus thrower pushes off his rear foot while planting his front foot, forcing his hips to rotate, but the rotation *continues* through the torso with the abdominal and back muscles.

Exercises that emphasize torso rotation are included in many sport-specific workout programs found later in the book.

and hip *abductions*. That's one-sixth the training time and equipment!

Athletes can choose from several multijoint exercises that effectively strengthen each basic movement. Equipment availability, respect for growth and development, and personal preference determine final exercise selection. Movement by movement, let's take a look at some possible choices.

PERSONALIZING THE SPORTS STRENGTH PROGRAM

Remember that you can work each basic movement through many different exercises and pieces of equipment; by selecting those recommended for your age or experience, you'll build a strong, injury-free foundation for years of successful strength training.

Personalizing your Sports Strength Program is easy: Select an equal number of exercises from each basic movement category. This ensures a training program that proportionally strengthens all the body's major muscle groups.

1. Examine the basic movement chart and select one exercise from each category. Be sure to follow the *yes* and *no* recommendations.
2. Write the selections on your strength-training chart.

Following are two sample Sports Strength Programs using the basic movement exercises.

SPORTS STRENGTH PROGRAM BASIC MOVEMENT CHART

Basic Movements		Adult & Late Adolescent	Beginner, Early Adolescence and Kids
Leg & Hip Thrust	Squat	Yes	No
	Leg Press	Yes	Yes
	Lunge	Yes	Yes
	Step-Ups	Yes	Yes
	Hack Squat	Yes	Maybe
Jackknife	Sit Ups	Yes	Yes
	Leg raises	Yes	Yes
Back Extension	Back Extension	Yes	Yes
	Good morning	Yes	No
	Stiff-Legged Barbell Deadlift	Yes	Yes
Upper Body Thrust	Bench press	Yes	Yes
	Dip	Yes	No
	Push Press	Yes	No
Upper Body Pull	Pull ups	Yes	Yes
	Lat Machine Pull downs	Yes	Yes
	Bent-over Dumbbell rows	Yes	No
	Seated Cable Long pulls	Yes	Yes
	Power Cleans	Yes	No

SPORTS STRENGTH TRAINING CHART

Name: Mike   Age: 19

Exercise	Page #	Sets	Reps	Lbs.
1. Squat	98	3	6	355
2. Sit Ups	103	3	10	20
3. Good Morning	106	3	6	115
4. Push Press	111	3	6	205
5. Power Cleans	116	3	6	225
6.				
7.				
8.				
9.				
10.				

SPORTS STRENGTH TRAINING CHART

Name: Katie   Age: 11

Exercise	Page #	Sets	Reps	Lbs.
1. Leg Press	99	2	10	200
2. Sit Ups	103	2	10	slant board
3. Back Extension	105	2	10	10
4. Bench Press	108	2	10	65
5. Pull Ups	112	2	10	—
6.				
7.				
8.				
9.				
10.				

The Sports Strength Program Exercises

BASIC MOVEMENT: LEG AND HIP THRUST

Primary muscle groups worked: Hips and thighs (gluteus maximus, gluteus medius, biceps femoris, vastus lateralis, vastus intermedius, vastus medialis, rectus femoris, semitendinosus, semimembranosus)

SQUAT

Training Tip: How low a squat? Many doctors recommend against bending the knee more than 90 degrees during a squat, but little, if any, evidence supports this idea. Squat as low as feels comfortable. Just keep your heels on the floor during the entire movement; this keeps the knees above the feet, preventing them from moving too far forward.

The beginner, early adolescent, and prepubescent should avoid squats. A weight heavy enough to adequately stress the legs and hips is too heavy for the inexperienced or growing shoulder girdle and back.

Correct Technique:

1. Stand with your feet shoulders-width apart, and the bar resting across the shoulders. Stabilize your torso by isometrically contracting the abdominals and back.
2. Keeping heels on the floor and your eyes forward, lower to the bottom position without bending the trunk forward more than 45 degrees.
3. Without stopping, bouncing, or jerking at the bottom position, drive up to the starting position in a smooth transition. Hold your breath throughout the movement; inhale and exhale at the top between repetitions.

LEG PRESS

Training Tips: Inhale while lowering the weight to the bottom position. Hold your breath as you drive the weight to the top of the movement, then exhale and repeat the sequence.

Sometimes athletic competition stresses the tendons attaching the quadriceps to the tibia and fibula. If sore knees interfere with your leg presses, move your feet forward on an inverted machine's foot pad (or a seated machine's top pad).

Correct Technique:

1. Lie on the backrest with your feet spaced 18 to 24 inches apart on the foot pad.
2. Press the weight to the top position and release the safety stops.
3. As you inhale, lower the weight to the bottom position, keeping knees bent 90 to 110 degrees.
4. Holding your breath, press the weight to the top position.
5. Keep the hips down and the lower back pressed against the backrest during the entire movement.

Variation: Substitute single-leg presses for the standard (double-leg) leg press every other workout. The training effect is markedly different. On the inverted leg press machine, slide your body to one side of the backrest to position your foot at the pad's center.

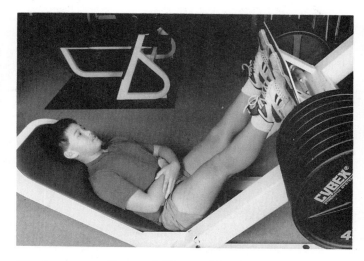

The leg press offers stability and back support that the squat lacks, making it an excellent strength-builder for all ages and experience levels.

LUNGE

Training Tip: Holding your heel on the ground keeps the knee above your foot as you drop into the low position.

Beginners: Practice correct form without weights for the first several workouts. Once you can perfectly execute ten reps with each leg without weight, add dumbbells. As balance improves, try a barbell.

The lunge works the calf muscles (gastrocnemius, soleus) in addition to the hips and thighs. Beginners should practice the movement without weights until they perfect their balance.

Correct Technique:

1. Stand upright with feet placed shoulders-width apart. Hold dumbbells at arm's length, palms facing toward thighs.
2. Keeping your head up and back straight, take a long step forward with either foot. Plant the foot and drop the hips until the lead thigh is parallel to the floor.
3. Push backward and upward with the lead foot until you are standing erect at the starting position.
4. Repeat with the opposite leg. That's one rep.

STEP-UPS

Safety Tip: Check your bench for stability before beginning.

Beginners: Perform the first workout without weights, perfecting your balance and form. Add one or two dumbbells after mastering the technique. In subsequent workouts, as your movement becomes more coordinated, you may use a barbell.

Correct Technique:

1. With feet together, face the *end* of the weight bench.
2. Step up with the right foot and stand erect on the bench.
3. Step down; start with the left leg and follow with the right.
4. Repeat the movement, stepping up with the *left* leg and continuing the sequence. That's one rep.
5. Alternate legs until you've completed the required reps. That's a set.

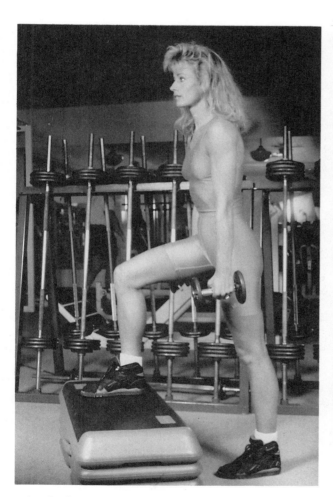

Like the lunge, step-ups work the calf muscles (gastrocnemius, soleus) as well as hips and thighs. Squats and leg presses don't.

The momentum of hanging dumbbells can strain the shoulders, especially for younger lifters. Instead, use one dumbbell twice as heavy, holding it rigidly against the front of the body.

HACK SQUAT

Training Tip: Correct placement on the foot pad depends on leg length. Taller athletes position the feet toward the front, shorter athletes toward the back. The object is to minimize knee stress when your thigh is perpendicular to the foot pad—the exercise's low position.

The athlete's shoulders might be too narrow to safety and effectively use this machine. Early-adolescent, female, and prepubescent athletes are often too weak in the lower back and shoulder girdle to endure the hack squat machine's leg and hip drive.

Correct Technique:

1. Facing away from the machine, position your shoulders under the shoulder pads, pressing your back against the back pad.
2. Stand erect while releasing the safety stops.
3. Inhale, lowering your body until your thighs are parallel to the foot pad.
4. With your back pressed against the pad, hold your breath as you return to the standing position. Exhale at the top. That's a rep.

BASIC MOVEMENT: JACKKNIFE

Primary muscle groups worked: Abdominals (rectus abdominis, internal obliques, external obliques, erector spinae, psoas, transversus abdominis)

SIT-UPS

Training Tip: Train your abdominals with heavy resistance and low reps, just as you strength-train other muscle groups.

Beginners: Add resistance by increasing the sit-up board's angle. When you can perform the required reps and sets at the highest angle, add weight, increasing the poundage as you can.

Correct Technique:
1. Lie on your back with hands clasped behind the neck. Hold a dumbbell if strength permits. Bend your knees.
2. Sit up slowly and smoothly, pausing momentarily at the top position.
3. Slowly return to the starting position, keeping knees bent throughout the movement. That's a rep.

STRENGTHEN THOSE ABS!

Arm, chest, shoulder, leg and abdominal muscles are made of the same fibers. Even under a microscope, they look identical.

Throughout this book, you've read that muscle grows stronger through progressive resistance training. That's a fact whether the muscle is in the arm or the abdomen. For this reason, use the same set/rep patterns when exercising your abdominals as when you're exercising your legs or chest. Few reps and heavy weights increase *strength*. High-repetition, low-resistance sets—twenty to one hundred or more reps with low or no weight—increase muscular *endurance*.

Even experienced strength athletes fall into a trap of high-repetition sit-ups and leg raises. It's a carryover from old bodybuilding maga-

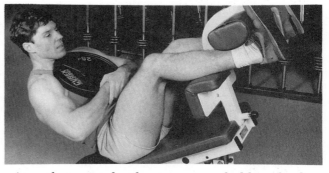

zines that mistakenly recommended hundreds of sit-ups to reduce the midsection.

A weak midsection is a major athletic liability. Every bend and trunk rotation involves contracting the abdominal muscles. And the only way leg power can reach the upper body is through the midsection.

LEG RAISES

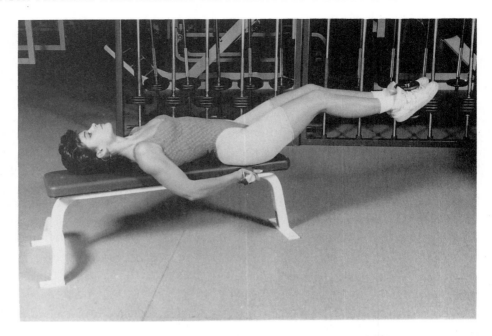

Training Tip: Perform leg raises with sets of low reps. Progressively increase resistance by holding a dumbbell between the feet, or using a cable pulley or resistance band.

Beginners: Leg raises are difficult for many at first. If you can't keep your legs straight, bend them as your strength level requires.

Correct Technique:

1. Lie with your back on the floor or a bench; extend your legs in line with your body.
2. Raise both legs simultaneously, keeping them straight, until the feet are above the hips.
3. Lower the legs to the starting position. That's a rep.

BASIC MOVEMENT: BACK EXTENSION

Primary muscle groups worked: Spinal erectors, deep posterior group (iliocostalis thoracis, multifidus, spinalis dorsi, longissimus thoracis, intertransversarti)

BACK EXTENSION

Practice progressive resistance training, increasing the weight whenever possible.

Training Tip: If you use a seated back machine with a selector stack, don't bounce or jerk during the exercise movement. Controlling the resistance helps avoid injury.

Correct Technique:

1. Lie facedown, extending your upper body over the end of a high bench. Place your feet under a support, or have a spotter apply pressure to keep you positioned. Clasp your hands or hold a dumbbell behind your head.
2. Keeping your back straight, bend at the waist until your torso is perpendicular to your legs.
3. Return to the starting position, maintaining a straight back throughout the movement's arc. Hold the starting position for one second. That's a rep.

GOOD MORNING

Training Tip: A bent knee is often necessary for balance during this exercise, but maintain pressure on the spinal erectors, bands of muscle running parallel to your spinal column, from the hips to the shoulder girdle.

Correct Technique:

1. Stand erect with your feet shoulders-width apart and a barbell positioned across your neck and shoulders. Steady the barbell with a wide grip on the bar.
2. Keeping your back straight and knees slightly bent, slowly bend forward until your torso is parallel with the floor.
3. Return through the same arc to the starting position. That's a rep.

Isolate the intended muscle group: Bend only at the waist, keeping the upper body rigid.

STIFF-LEGGED BARBELL DEADLIFT

Training Tip: If you're flexible enough, stand on a low platform to extend the movement several additional inches.

Beginners: To protect your lower back, perform the exercise slowly, taking care not to bounce the weight at the bottom of the exercise.

Correct Technique:

1. Stand with a barbell at arm's length, keeping feet parallel and shoulders-width apart. Grasp the bar several inches wider than shoulders-width.
2. Keeping knees slightly bent, back straight, and head up, bend forward at the waist until the barbell touches the floor.
3. Return through the same arc to the starting position. That's a rep.

BASIC MOVEMENT: UPPER-BODY THRUST
Primary muscle groups worked: Chest, shoulder girdle, triceps

BENCH PRESS

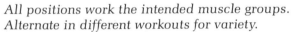
All positions work the intended muscle groups. Alternate in different workouts for variety.

Training Tips: Flat, incline, and decline positions all develop upper-body pushing power. As a general recommendation, alternate flat and incline positions with each workout to vary the stress and broaden the muscular adaptation.

Hand spacing is another important variable. Don't use just your strongest hand placement; multiple positions increase the probability that the added strength will apply to your athletic movements. Remember, don't perform free-weight chest presses without a spotter.

Use a U-shaped bar if you have access to one. You'll need to use a lighter weight until your muscles develop strength through the greater range of motion.

Beginners: If it fits your body, you can substitute a machine for a barbell until you've developed more confidence and coordination. As with a barbell, vary the hand spacing and press angle with each workout.

Correct Technique:

1. Plant your feet firmly on the floor. Place hands shoulders-width apart, supporting the bar at arm's length.
2. Point the elbows out and keep the bar under control as you lower it to your chest. The bar should touch the chest an inch above the nipples if you use a flat bench, high on the chest with an incline bench, or below the nipples on a decline bench.
3. Press the bar up until your arms are fully extended at the starting position. That's a rep.

Incline position.

Decline position.

DIP

Training Tip: If your equipment is adjustable, vary the dip bar's angle or change your hand placement with each workout.

Beginners: If you aren't strong enough to complete a set without assistance, have a spotter support your ankles—applying only the force necessary to complete each rep. As always, be careful not to bounce or jerk at the low point. Control the movement throughout the exercise.

The dip is not recommended for beginners, prepubescents, or early-adolescent athletes.

Correct Technique:
1. Start by supporting yourself on dip bars. Keep your arms straight and shoulders-width apart, your body erect, and your eyes forward.
2. Bend your elbows, lowering your body with control until your shoulder muscles feel a stretch. If the bars are straight, your elbows should point straight back; if the dip bars are angled, the elbows should follow the angle.
3. Press upward until you reach the starting position. That's a rep.

PUSH PRESS

Training Tip: The spine should remain in a normal standing position throughout the exercise movement. Look straight forward while pushing the barbell overhead to maintain correct posture.

Beginners: Approach this exercise with caution; it is essential to avoid overarching the back to prevent injuries. Don't overload the bar at the expense of correct form.

Correct Technique:

1. Assume the position by either power-cleaning (refer to the power-clean exercise description later in this chapter) the barbell to your shoulders, or stepping under a barbell positioned on a power rack. Keep feet parallel and shoulders-width apart.
2. Start the movement by squatting approximately 30 to 45 degrees. Immediately thrust the legs straight, accelerating the barbell upward. Continue the barbell's acceleration by pushing until your arms are fully extended. The exercise is an explosive, continuous, leg/arm thrust sequence.
3. Momentarily pause at the top. Control the barbell as you lower it to the starting position. That's a rep.

The push press—requiring leg, hip, torso, shoulder, and arm coordination—is the recommended upper-body thrust movement for experienced adults and late-adolescent athletes. Beginner, early-adolescent, and prepubescent athletes should avoid the push press.

BASIC MOVEMENT: UPPER-BODY PULL

Primary muscle groups worked: Upper back, biceps, chest, shoulder girdle (latissimus dorsi, pectoralis major, teres major, rhomboid, pectoralis minor, trapezius)

PULL-UPS

Training Tips: Many athletes incorrectly abbreviate the exercise movement. Correct technique demands a complete arm, shoulder, and lat stretch in the low position.

You should also vary the hand spacing between workouts, producing an expanded adaptation range.

Beginners: If you can't perform a complete set of pull-ups, have someone assist by supporting your ankles, allowing you to push with your leg muscles just enough to complete each rep.

Correct Technique:

1. Using an overhand grip, hang from the bar as low as possible, stretching the lats, arms, and shoulders.
2. Pull your body up eye-level with the bar.
3. Lower to the starting position. That's a rep.

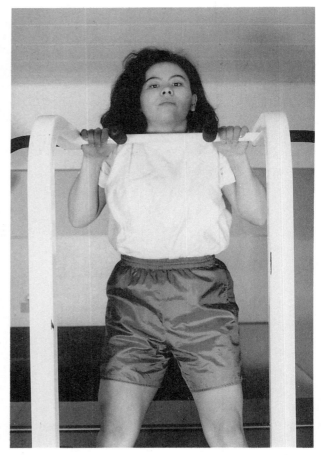

LAT MACHINE PULL-DOWNS

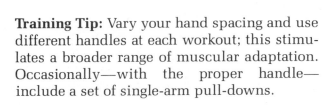

The pull-down and pull-up are equivalent movements. Alternate them for workout variety.

Training Tip: Vary your hand spacing and use different handles at each workout; this stimulates a broader range of muscular adaptation. Occasionally—with the proper handle—include a set of single-arm pull-downs.

Correct Technique:

1. Sitting with your legs under a bracing bar, pull the bar down until it touches the top of your chest.
2. Using control, return the bar to the starting position. That's a rep.

BENT-OVER DUMBBELL ROW

Training Tip: Working with dumbbells rather than a barbell increases the range of motion, building a greater strength range for athletic movements.

Correct Technique:

1. Position your left knee and hand on a bench; keep your back straight and parallel with the floor. The dumbbell hangs from your right arm.

2. Point your elbow toward the ceiling as you pull the dumbbell to your shoulder.
3. Lower the dumbbell toward the floor, fully stretching your upper back, shoulder, and arm at the low position. That's a rep.
4. After completing a set, switch positions and repeat the exercise for the left side.

SEATED CABLE LONG PULLS

Training Tip: The long pull's one-arm exercise involves a torso rotation that does not occur with the more rigidly controlled two-arm version. If you opt for two-arm long pulls, vary the movement by interchanging handles with each workout. Most gyms have several bars and handles that can be attached to the cable machine.

Beginners: Control the weight throughout the motion. Don't accelerate the weight with a jerk at the beginning, or allow the weight's momentum to overstretch your lower back at the movement's end.

Correct Technique:

1. Start the exercise with your torso at a 45-degree angle to the floor. The arm, shoulder, and side of the upperback working the cable should stretch forward to resist the weight's pull.
2. Simultaneously straighten and rotate your torso while pulling, until the pulley handle touches the rib cage. Your torso should be perpendicular to the floor, and your working shoulder rotated to the rear.
3. Return to the starting position: arm stretched forward and torso at a 45-degree angle to the floor. That's a rep.

Early-adolescent and pre-pubescent athletes should replace the power clean with the long pull.

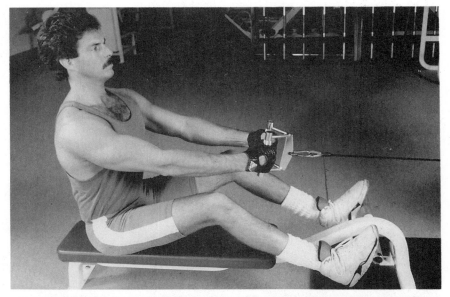

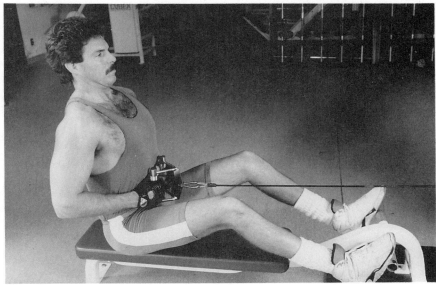

POWER CLEANS

Training Tip: Heavy power cleans require mastering the pull's leg/hip/arm sequence. The powerful leg and lower-back muscles initiate the pull, accelerating the barbell so that the less powerful upper-body muscles can complete the movement.

Beginners: Although it's tempting to bounce the barbell, each repetition should begin from a total stop with arms straight.

Correct Technique:

1. Stand with your feet 16 inches apart, shins touching the bar. Bend down and grip the bar overhand. Position upper legs parallel to the floor, straighten the back, and look forward.
2. Begin the exercise movement by straightening your legs, maintaining straight arms as the barbell rises from the floor.

3. As the legs straighten, extend the hips forward, initiating an erect posture. The arms begin to bend at this point.
4. As the body straightens, continue the bar's ascent by simultaneously pulling with the arms and rising on the toes.
5. When the bar reaches its highest point, bend the knees, catching the bar on the shoulders and upper chest. Stand fully.
6. Control the bar as you lower it to the floor. That's a rep.

Once you've mastered your Sports Strength Program, you may want to do more to meet your sport's specific challenges. In chapter 12, skill-performance training programs focus on common athletic actions: jumping, leg speed, hand strength, swinging, and overhand throwing.

This movement's explosiveness makes it the best overall upper-body pulling exercise for experienced late-adolescent and adult athletes.

CHAPTER ELEVEN

SUPPLEMENTARY EXERCISES

BARBELL DEADLIFT

Training Tip: Correct technique demands that the weight remain close to (or touching) the body so that the back is not the primary mover. It is vital to straighten the legs and extend the hips as you raise the weight, and bend the hip and knee as you lower the bar. Look forward throughout the exercise.

Beginners: Don't jerk the weight from the floor, or bounce the weight between reps. Form is critical in this exercise. Lower the poundage rather than jeopardize your safety.

Correct Technique:

1. Start with your feet shoulders'-width apart, shins touching the bar, toes pointed 20 degrees outward, and your hands gripping the bar overhand. Bend your knees until your thighs are parallel to the floor. Look straight ahead.
2. Pull the barbell upward, simultaneously straightening your legs and extending the hips forward until your body is erect; keep the bar as close to your body as possible. When you stand straight, the barbell will be resting against the thighs.
3. Looking forward, simultaneously bend the hips and knees as the bar is returned to the floor. Maintain control throughout the exercise, and keep the bar close to your body. That's a rep.

BARBELL HIGH-PULL

Training Tip: Mastering the pull's leg/hip/arm sequence is necessary to executing the barbell high-pull correctly. The powerful leg and lower-back muscles initiate the pull, accelerating the barbell so that the less powerful upper-body muscles can complete the motion. Remember to change the width of the hand spacing with each workout.

Beginners: Don't bounce the barbell. Bring each repetition to a total stop with arms straight.

Correct Technique:

1. Stand with your feet 16 inches apart, shins touching the bar. Bend down and grip the bar overhand. Bend your knees until the upper legs are parallel to the floor. Keep your back straight and your eyes looking forward. That's the starting position.
2. Straighten the legs, keeping the arms straight as the barbell rises from the floor.
3. As your legs straighten, extend the hips forward. The arms should remain straight.
4. As your body reaches an erect posture, simultaneously pull with the arms and rise on the toes until the bar reaches the highest possible point. Unlike the power cleans, the elbows remain above the bar.
5. Control the bar by resisting gravity as you lower the barbell to the floor. That's a rep.

BARBELL OR DUMBBELL SHOULDER SHRUG

Beginners: Don't involve your lower back and legs by dipping the weight at the beginning of movement. The exercise is designed to strengthen the trapezius and upper back.

Correct Technique:

1. Stand erect, holding the barbell or a pair of dumbbells with an overhand grip. Hands should be shoulders-width apart; keep arms straight.
2. Raise your shoulders as high as possible while keeping the arms straight.
3. Lower your shoulders to the starting position. That's a rep.

Shoulder shrug with barbell.

Shoulder shrug with dumbbells.

STANDING ALTERNATE DUMBBELL PRESS

Training Tip: Accelerate the weight at the movement's beginning by slightly dipping and thrusting the shoulder during alternate reps. Bodybuilders isolate the shoulder by keeping the upper body rigid, but that technique is inappropriate for developing synchronous athletic movements.

Correct Technique:

1. With legs and hips locked, press one dumbbell to arm's length.

2. Lower the dumbbell to the shoulder, simultaneously pressing the opposite dumbbell to arm's length.
3. Lower the second dumbbell and repeat the sequence.

Variation: Include the seated version for a psychological boost on a lethargic day.

TOE RAISE: SEATED CALF MACHINE

Correct Technique:

1. Sit on the machine's seat, or on a bench with a barbell atop your knees.
2. Lower your heels as low as possible, stretching your calf muscles. This is the starting point.
3. Flex your calves, rising on the toes as high as possible.
4. Using control, return to the heels-low position. That's a rep.

TOE RAISE: LEG PRESS MACHINE

Correct Technique:

1. Leave the safety stops in place if they don't restrict your movement. Lie (or sit if using a seated machine) on the back support with the balls of your feet pressed against the foot pad. Press upward until your legs are straight and your knees are locked. Allow your calves to stretch. This is the starting position.
2. Press up on your toes until your foot is fully extended.
3. Lower the rack with control until you return to the starting position. That's a rep.

TOE RAISE: STANDING

Beginners: The untrained shoulders and torso cannot comfortably and safely support too much extra weight. Hence, the standing toe raise is not appropriate for beginners, particularly pubescents who haven't completed their growth spurts.

Correct Technique:

1. Using a power rack, place a barbell on your shoulders. Stand erect, eyes forward, with the balls of your feet on a broad, stable board approximately 2 inches high. Stretch your calves by lowering the heels. That's the starting position.
2. Rise up on the toes as high as possible, momentarily holding the calf muscles' contraction at the top.
3. Using control, lower your heels to the stretched-calf starting position. That's a rep.

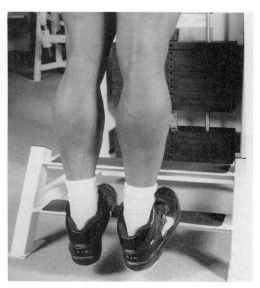

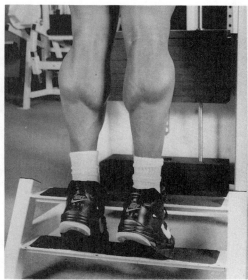

DUMBBELL BENCH-FLY

Variation: Change the bench angles with each workout, but spend the most time on the angle that is closest to your particular athletic movement.

Beginners: The fly is not an easy movement; beginners often lose control of the dumbbells. Use a light weight for several workouts until you master the form.

Correct Technique:

1. Lie on a flat, incline, or decline bench, with your feet flat on the floor. Hold the dumbbells at arm's length above the shoulders, palms facing each other as the dumbbells nearly touch.
2. Lower the dumbbells through arcs until the shoulders and chest are comfortably stretched. The elbows can bend as much as 45 degrees while lowering the dumbbells.
3. Return the dumbbells through the same semicircular path, being careful not to bang them. That's a rep.

BENT-ARM DUMBBELL PULLOVER

Training Tip: Select a bench that permits full exercise movement without the dumbbells reaching the floor. Don't bounce or jerk the weight from the floor between reps. And keep your elbows close together next to your body throughout the motion.

Alternative Equipment: Pullover machines can occasionally substitute for dumbbell pull-overs. Perform the exercise by pulling on the bar; avoid the elbow pads completely.

Correct Technique:

1. Lie on a flat bench with your head extending over one end and your feet on the floor. Hold a dumbbell in each hand, palms in.
2. Keeping your elbow close to your body, lower one dumbbell in an arc from your chest until the shoulder is fully stretched. Keep the arm bent and the back flat against the bench.
3. Return the dumbbell to the chest through the same arc, completing the movement before repeating with the opposite arm. That's one rep.

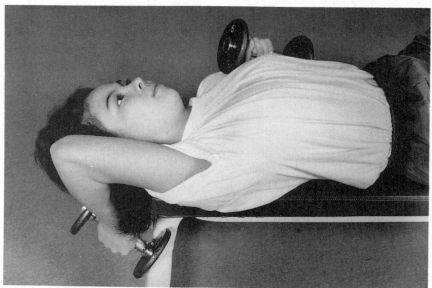

STRAIGHT-ARM PULLOVER

Training Tip: Drop your hips below the bench level to fully stretch your rib cage.

Correct Technique:

1. Lie across a flat bench, head extended over the side. Hold one end of a dumbbell at arm's length above the shoulder; keep elbows as close together as possible.
2. Lower the dumbbell in a semicircular path toward the floor, stretching within a painless range.
3. Return along the same path to the starting position. That's a rep.

Variation: Perform the barbell version of the exercise in the same way. Grip the barbell in the center, hands spaced approximately 6 inches apart.

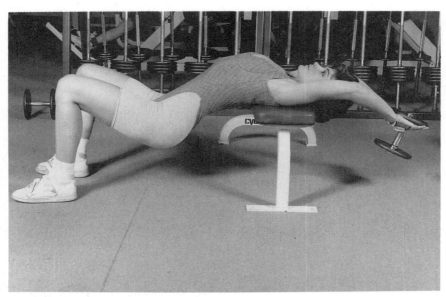

LOW-PULLEY LEG PULL-IN

Variation: If you have the luxury of a well-equipped gym, practice all forms of the basic exercise movement, interchanging the pulley, leg curl machine, and standing leg machine with each workout.

Correct Technique:

1. Lie on your back with both legs straight, one ankle strapped to a pulley cable. Brace the opposite foot to avoid sliding toward the machine.
2. Bend the leg attached to the cable, pulling the knee toward your chest as far as possible.
3. Using control, return your foot to the starting position. Repeat the required number of reps, and switch legs.

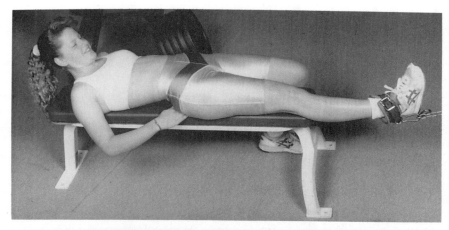

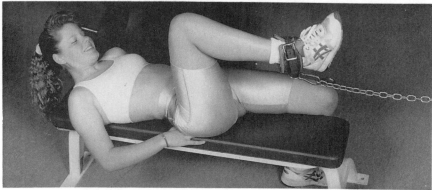

Alternative Equipment: You can perform the movement with one or both legs on the leg curl machine; position your body as pictured. To perform the exercise while standing, pull the knee as high as possible and lower the weight with control.

LEG CURL

Training Tip: Keep your hips pressed against the bench to ensure the hamstrings' full range of motion.

Correct Technique:

1. Lie facedown on the machine, positioning the leg pad at the back of the ankles.

2. Without jerking or raising your hips, bend your knees while concentrating on the hamstrings' contraction.

3. Using control, lower to the starting position. That's a rep.

Variation: Perform the exercise one leg at a time.

KNEE EXTENSION

Correct Technique:

1. Without jerking to accelerate the weight, straighten your legs until your knees are extended to just short of the locked position.

2. Lower your legs to the starting position, completely stopping at the bottom. That's a rep.

Variation: Try single-leg knee extensions.

WRIST CURL

Training Tip: A dumbbell restricts less than a barbell, permitting more natural motion.

Correct Technique:

1. Sit with the back of your wrist stabilized on the knee and the elbow against the thigh. Hold the dumbbell with a secure palms-up grip and let your hand and dumbbell hang toward the floor.

2. Curl the dumbbell as high as possible by contracting the forearm muscles.
3. Keeping the elbow on the thigh, lower the dumbbell to the starting position. That's a rep.

Variation: Induce greater muscular adaptation by occasionally holding the dumbbell perpendicular to the floor.

WRIST EXTENSION

Correct Technique:
1. Sit with the back of the wrist stabilized on the knee and the elbow against the thigh. Grip the dumbbell palms-down, and let your hand and dumbbell hang to the floor.
2. Curl the dumbbell as high as possible by contracting the forearm muscles.
3. Keeping the elbow on the thigh and wrist on the knee, lower the dumbbell to the starting position. That's a rep.

ALTERNATING UPRIGHT ROWS

Correct Technique:

1. Stand erect with your feet shoulders-width apart, dumbbells hanging at your sides, and palms facing your body.
2. Pull the dumbbell up along your body, keeping your elbow higher than the dumbbell throughout the movement. At the top of the movement, the dumbbell should be positioned at the front of the shoulder, with your elbow up.
3. Lower the dumbbell with control to the starting position.
4. Repeat the movement with the opposite arm.

ALTERNATING DUMBBELL BENCH PRESS

Training Tip: Dumbbells permit a more natural pressing movement and a greater range of motion than a barbell. For an athlete, the dumbbell bench press is the superior exercise.

Correct Technique:

1. Lie on a flat incline or decline bench at the angle most appropriate for your athletic movement. Stabilize the dumbbells at your shoulders, with palms facing your body and feet spaced wide and flat on the floor.
2. Press one dumbbell to arm's length, allowing the palm to naturally rotate forward during the movement.
3. Lower the dumbbell to the shoulder and repeat the movement with the opposite arm.

CABLE PULLEY OVERHAND THROW

Training Tips: Attaching the cable to your wrist rather than your hand lets you use a heavier weight while mimicking your natural throwing motion. The throwing motion tends to suffer when gripping a pulley handle. Any hand and wrist strength training lost by not gripping the pulley can be replaced with specific exercises.

The exercise's focus is strength development in the shoulder girdle and arm. The normal leg, hip, and torso motions are part of the exercise, but you must modulate their force to allow the shoulder girdle and arm to safely and effectively perform the exercise.

Successfully throwing a baseball, football, javelin, or softball depends on subtly different throwing motions. Approximate your sport's throwing motion as closely as possible when performing this exercise. The accompanying photographs and explanatory text are generalizations that you should adapt to your specific technique.

Beginners: Start with a very light weight. Slowly increase the resistance with each workout, protecting your shoulder and arm until you have mastered your sport's specific form.

Correct Technique:

1. Strap the cable to your wrist. Stand or sit, bracing yourself so that the cable's opposing force does not compromise your balance.
2. Duplicate your sport-specific throwing motion; be certain that the range of motion is complete.
3. Return to the starting position, taking care to control the weight throughout the return.

CABLE PULLEY SWING

Training Tip: Try to mimic your sport's swing when performing this exercise. The accompanying photographs and explanatory text are generalized instructions.

Beginners: Start with an obviously light weight. Slowly increase the weight with each workout, protecting your shoulder and arm until you have mastered your sport's form.

Correct Technique:

1. Strap the cable to your wrist or use an appropriate handle. Stand, bracing yourself if necessary so that the cable's opposing force does not compromise your balance.
2. Duplicate your sport-specific swinging motion, moving the cable under control.
3. Return to the starting position, taking care to control the weight throughout the return.

DUMBBELL BICEPS CURL

Correct Technique:

1. Stand, or sit on an inclined or flat bench. Hang the dumbbells to your sides, palms facing toward the body.
2. Without swinging the dumbbell to enhance acceleration, curl one of the dumbbells through an arc to your chin. The elbow remains down, the upper arm remains pressed to the body, and the palm turns upward through the movement.
3. Lower the dumbbell through the same arc. Repeat with the opposite arm.

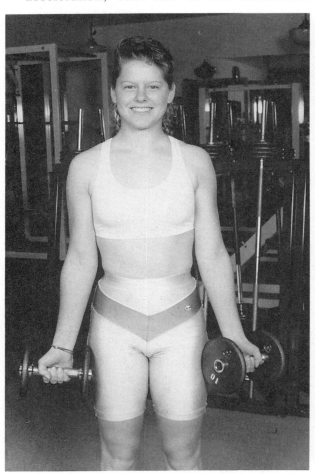 

TRICEPS EXTENSION

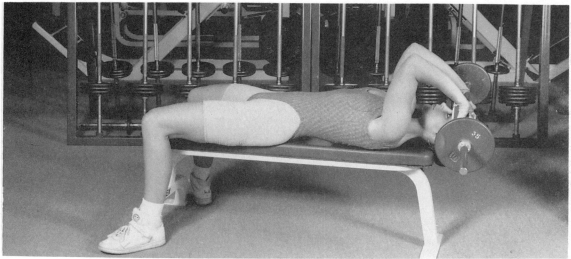

Training Tip: There are many versions of the triceps extension. The important thing is to let your triceps do the work. Don't jerk or "kick" the weight for acceleration, which might produce enough force to overstretch the elbow ligaments.

Correct Technique:

1. Lie on your back. Grip a barbell with your palms up and your hands spaced 6 to 12 inches apart. Hold the barbell at arm's length above your shoulders.

2. Keeping your upper arm perpendicular to your torso, lower the bar through an arc until the backs of your hands touch your forehead.

3. Return the barbell through the arc to the starting position, keeping the upper arm perpendicular to your torso throughout the movement. That's a rep.

ROTATOR CUFF SERIES

Training Tip: This exercise set is particularly valuable to athletes who rely on overhand throws, especially quarterbacks, pitchers, and javelin throwers. The exercises strengthen the muscles that stabilize the shoulder, helping to prevent career-threatening rotator cuff injuries.

Exercise One

1. Lie with your back on the floor, elbow at your side, and hand gripping a dumbbell positioned as shown.

2. Lift the dumbbell through an arc until your hand is directly above your elbow. Keep your upper arm and elbow on the floor throughout the lift.

3. Lower the dumbbell to the floor through the same arc. That's a rep.

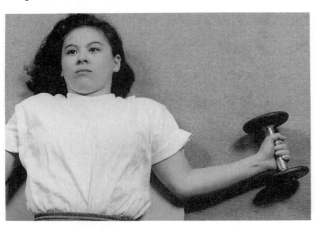 

Exercise Two

1. Lie on your side, elbow pressed against you, and your hand gripping a dumbbell positioned on the floor as shown.

2. Lift the dumbbell through an arc until your forearm is parallel to the floor. Keep your upper arm and elbow pressed against your side throughout the lift.

3. Lower the dumbbell to the floor through the same arc. That's a rep.

Exercise Three

1. Lie on your back on the floor, with your upper arm at a 90-degree angle to your body. Grip a dumbbell positioned above your head as pictured.
2. Keeping the elbow at a right angle and the arm pressed against the floor, move the dumbbell through a 180-degree arc until the dumbbell touches the floor at the side of your hip.
3. Return the dumbbell through the same arc to the starting position. That's a rep.

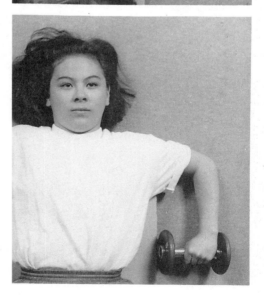

REVERSE TRUNK TWIST

Training Tip: The reverse trunk twist is the most basic exercise to strengthen the muscles responsible for torso rotation. As your ability improves, the resistance can be increased sequentially by straightening the legs, and thereafter adding ankle weights to the straightened legs.

Correct Technique:

1. Lie with your back on the floor, arms extended to your sides, knees bent, and your thighs vertical.

2. Slowly lower your knees to one side of your body, keeping the thighs perpendicular to your torso as they touch the floor.
3. Return to the starting position and lower your thighs to the opposite side.
4. Return the thighs to the vertical position. That's a rep.

BARBELL PLATE TWIST

Correct Technique:

1. Stand erect with a barbell plate held at arm's length to the front of your chest.
2. Slowly twist your torso to one side, keeping the barbell plate at arm's length in front of the chest.
3. Return to the starting position and twist your torso to the opposite side.
4. Return to the starting position. That's a rep.

BENT-ARM FRONT RAISE

Correct Technique:

1. Stand erect with your feet shoulders-width apart, dumbbells hanging at your sides and palms facing your body.
2. Keeping the elbow bent approximately 30 degrees throughout the movement, raise one dumbbell through an arc to the front of the body until reaching shoulder height.
3. Return the dumbbell to the starting position.
4. Duplicate the movement with the opposite arm. That's a rep.

PLYOMETRIC DEPTH JUMP

Training Tip: If depth jumps are new for you, start at a low height. Progressively increase the height of the box as your body adapts to the stress of the exercise over weeks and months of training.

Correct Technique:

1. From the top of a sturdy box, drop to the floor landing on both feet.
2. Immediately upon landing, jump to the top of another lower, sturdy box. That's a rep.

FROG HOP

The frog hop begins and ends on the floor and is safer for the beginner than the more rigorous depth jump. Because of the additional forces generated from the drop of the depth jump, stick with frog hops until you can leg press twice your body weight or squat with 150% of your body weight.

CHAPTER TWELVE

SPECIALIZED PERFORMANCE PROGRAMS

How should I strength-train to throw farther and faster? How can I jump higher? What will help my swing? Can I improve my leg speed? How can I tighten my grip? These are athletes' most common strength-training questions. Here are the answers:

Most athletic events depend on a sum of muscular forces, often beginning at the feet and peaking at the fingertips. Any weak link along the way reduces the total force.

These programs are for you if your hands are your weak link, for example, or if you need to specifically strengthen the muscles of your jump, run, swing, or throw.

JUMPS

Mark Henry, an American champion super-heavyweight weight lifter, weighs 370 pounds, yet can still dunk a basketball!

The jumper's training goal is to strengthen the muscles used in the jump. The muscles will then put out more power, increasing explosive movements. (Review "How Does Strength Training Build Power?" in chapter 1.)

If better jumping is your only strength-training goal, avoid gains except in muscles directly contributing to the jump. That's because jumping is an antigravity event—each extra ounce of body weight is that much more to lift against the downward pull.

The Muscles of Jumping

The leg and hip muscles obviously propel the jump, but the shoulders, abdomen, and back are also very important.

THE MUSCLES AND CORRESPONDING
EXERCISE MOVEMENTS OF JUMPING

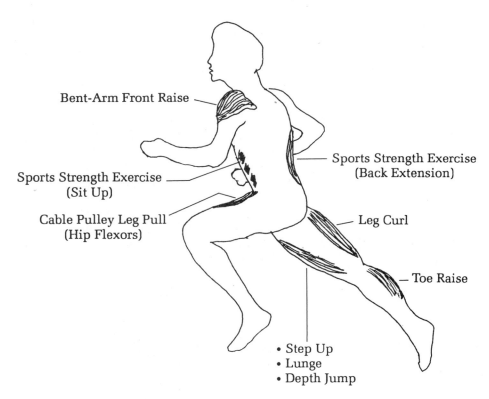

Bent-Arm Front Raise

Sports Strength Exercise
(Sit Up)

Cable Pulley Leg Pull
(Hip Flexors)

Sports Strength Exercise
(Back Extension)

Leg Curl

Toe Raise

• Step Up
• Lunge
• Depth Jump

JUMP PROGRAM

* The step-up or lunge is in addition to the hip and leg thrust movement(s) already in your Sports Strength Program.

Adults/Late Adolescents

Off-Season: Two or three training days per week, per exercise. Follow the set/rep patterns outlined in the periodization schedule on page 79.

In-Season: Two sets of six repetitions at 80 percent of 1RM, two or three training days per week, per exercise.

Kids/Early Adolescents

First-Year Program: Perform two sets of ten repetitions at 65 percent of 1RM, two days per week throughout the year.

Second-Year Program: Begin a modified off-season periodization schedule as outlined on page 79 after completing the first year of a strength-training program.

Bent-Arm Front Raise

The benefits of the shoulder and arm thrust to the jump are twofold: they add upward momentum, and the arms' elevation raises the body's center of gravity.

Cable Pulley Leg Pull

This exercise strengthens the muscles that pull your knee skyward, increasing knee drive during the takeoff.

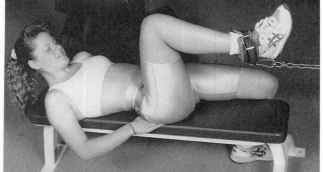

Toe Raise

The toe raise strengthens the calf muscles—the soleus and gastrocnemius—that explosively extend the ankle joint as the jumper leaves the ground.

Knee Curl

The knee curl is recommended as a safety precaution, to balance the hamstrings' muscular development with the quadriceps'. A quadricep/hamstring strength ratio of sixty pounds to forty pounds will prevent injury. For example, an athlete who can lift sixty pounds in the knee extension should be able to knee-curl forty pounds.

Step-up or Lunge

This exercise primarily strengthens the quadriceps, which straighten the knee of the takeoff leg. The stronger the quads, the greater the leg power.

Plyometric Frog Hop and Depth Jump

The frog hop rapidly stretches the jumping muscles upon landing, immediately followed by an explosive contraction on takeoff. This rapid stretch-explosion sequence produces up to 150 percent of the force that can be produced during normal weight training without prior stretching.

Frog hops and the more difficult depth jumps (pictured) are excellent jump developers, but because of the forces generated, don't attempt the depth jump until you can leg-press twice your body weight or squat with 150 percent of your body weight.

LEG SPEED

Many athletes assume that they can't improve the speed they were born with. That's just not true. Strength training does improve leg speed. Stronger muscles increase the running stride's frequency and length.

The number of fast-twitch muscle fibers and basic neural structure *are* a large component of speed. But strength training can make any athlete faster, moving him or her closer to that genetic potential.

The Muscles of Leg Speed

Most of the body's skeletal muscles directly or indirectly contribute to sprinting—some more than others. We're going to focus on the most important: the leg, hip, and midsection muscles.

THE MUSCLES AND APPROPRIATE
EXERCISES OF LEG SPEED

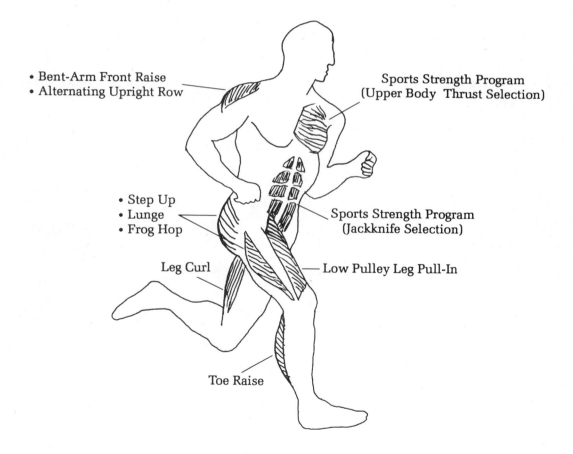

- Bent-Arm Front Raise
- Alternating Upright Row

Sports Strength Program
(Upper Body Thrust Selection)

- Step Up
- Lunge
- Frog Hop

Sports Strength Program
(Jackknife Selection)

Leg Curl

Low Pulley Leg Pull-In

Toe Raise

LEG SPEED PROGRAM

Adults/Late Adolescents

Off-Season: Two or three training days per week, per exercise. Follow the set/rep patterns outlined in the periodization schedule on page 79.

In-Season: Two sets of six repetitions at 80 percent of 1RM, two or three training days per week, per exercise.

Kids/Early Adolescents

First-Year Program: Perform two sets of ten repetitions at 65 percent of 1RM, two days per week throughout the year.
Second-Year Program: Begin a modified off-season periodization schedule as outlined on page 79 after completing the first year of a strength-training program.

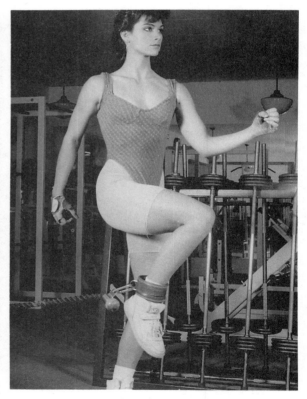

Low-Pulley Leg Pull-In

This exercise strengthens the hip flexors, increasing the knee's lift speed during the sprint; mimic that motion as closely as possible during the low-pulley leg pull-in.

Toe Raise

The toe raise strengthens ankle motion through the sprint's drive phase.

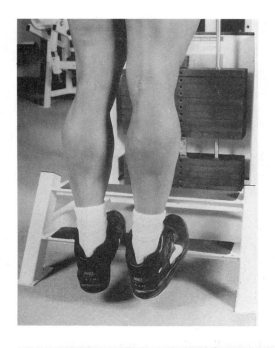

Step-up and Front Lunge

The step-up and front lunge strengthen the muscles primarily responsible for the leg drive that explosively straightens the hip and knee as the foot contacts the ground.

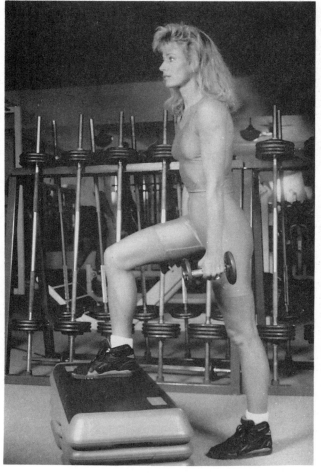

Leg Curl

The leg curl is essential for sprinters, because the knee's explosive extension while sprinting can overwhelm a weak hamstring. Leg curls strengthen the hamstrings, preventing many sprint-related injuries.

Bent-Arm Front Raise

The arms and shoulders contribute to much of the sprinter's technique and force.

Depth Jump with Horizontal Rebound

Varying the standard depth jump by including a horizontal thrust more closely approximates sprinting's actual stresses.

GRIP

Merely gripping barbells and dumbbells during a workout won't adequately strengthen the hands, wrists, and forearms for the majority of athletic events.

Imagine a deadlift, curl, or bench press. During each of these movements, the muscles largely controlling the hands, wrists, and forearms are *statically contracted*—not lengthening or shortening. But most athletes depend on *dynamic contractions* of those same muscles during intricate sports movements. For example, controlling a ball's flight would be impossible without dynamic contractions of the hand muscles during the throw.

Gripping Muscles

Twenty-seven bones, twenty-odd joints, and thirty-three muscles interact to control wrist, finger, and hand movement.

Hand strength is often crucial to athletic success. Consider the following:

For the thrower, the fingers are the last link in a chain of muscular force that begins at the foot, travels the length of the body, and propels a ball, javelin, discus, or shot across the field.

A stronger grip allows more of the body's force to transfer to a tennis racquet, baseball bat, fencing foil, or golf club. Increasing individual finger strength improves manipulative ability and consequent control when releasing a football, bowling ball, horseshoe, or basketball.

GRIP PROGRAM

Page Exercises
130   1. Wrist Curl
131   2. Wrist Extension
155   3. Rubber Balls or Rings

Adults/Late Adolescents

Off-Season: Two or three training days per week, per exercise. Follow the set/rep patterns outlined in the periodization schedule on page 79.

In-Season: Two sets of six repetitions at 80 percent of 1RM, two or three training days per week, per exercise.

Kids/Early Adolescents

First-Year Program: Perform two sets of ten repetitions at 65 percent of 1RM, two days per week throughout the year.

Second-Year Program: Begin a modified off-season periodization schedule as outlined on page 79 after completing one year of a strength-training program.

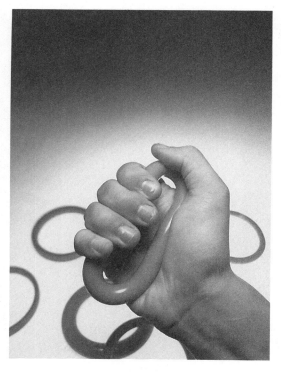

Dumbbell Wrist Extension and Curl

Dumbbell wrist extensions and curls dynamically exercise the muscles controlling wrist movement, but only statically exercise the hand's eleven muscles. These are essential exercises, but supplement them with dynamic exercises for the individual fingers.

Strength Rings

These rings, available in nine different tensions, can be used for exercising most finger movements—extensions as well as flexions. Exer-Rings™ cost about thirty dollars. Write to: 616 Enterprise Drive, Oakbrook, IL 60521, for more information.

Rubber Balls

Flexion exercises are illustrated at the right. The flexion exercises can be performed with rubber balls or strength rings. Rubber balls are available in various sizes from most toy stores. Although not as versatile as Exer-Rings™, several dollars buys a set.

SWING

The golf swing. The baseball swing. Racquet sports' backhand swings. All are technically different, but success in each depends on the same basic muscle groups, and similar biomechanics.

Strength training improves the swing's speed, resulting in greater potential distance for the ball. Strength training also improves the swing's control through better manipulation of the bat, club, or racket, improving accuracy.

Swinging Muscles

Tennis and racquetball backhands are powered by the same muscles as those used in the golf or baseball swing. Let's look:

THE MUSCLES OF SWING

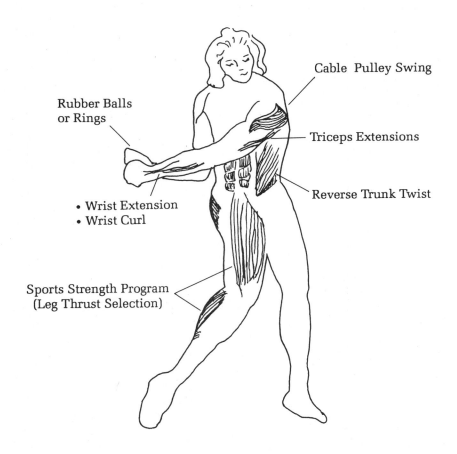

Cable Pulley Swing

Triceps Extensions

Reverse Trunk Twist

Rubber Balls or Rings

• Wrist Extension
• Wrist Curl

Sports Strength Program
(Leg Thrust Selection)

SWING PROGRAM

Adults/Late Adolescents

Off-Season: Two or three training days per week, per exercise. Follow the set/rep patterns outlined in the periodization schedule on page 79.

In-Season: Two sets of six repetitions at 80 percent of 1RM, two or three training days per week, per exercise.

Kids/Early Adolescents

First-Year Program: Perform two sets of ten repetitions at 65 percent of 1RM, two days per week throughout the year.
Second-Year Program: Begin a modified off-season periodization schedule as outlined on page 79 after completing one year of a strength-training program.

Cable Pulley Swing

Duplicate your sport-specific swing as closely as possible. Use a high, medium, or low pulley depending on the angle of motion. The photograph demonstrates the exercise as applied to a golf swing.

Triceps Extension

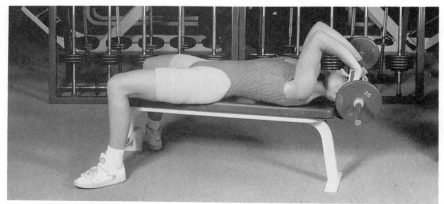

Reverse Trunk Twist

Strength-trained athletes often neglect these rotational exercises, but the twist strengthens the trunk rotation that is part of every swing.

Wrist Curl, Wrist Extension, Rings

A full transfer of muscular force from body to ball isn't possible without a strong grip on the bat, club, or racquet. Strengthen your grip with the exercises demonstrated below. Check the exercise descriptions earlier in the book for thorough technique explanations.

OVERHAND THROWS

Success in throwing the baseball, football, basketball, or javelin depends on much the same principle as the swing: The stronger the muscles, the faster the hand moves, and the harder or farther the object is thrown.

Regardless of the sport, most muscle groups are involved in a synchronous throwing motion. Of course, throwing techniques differ from sport to sport—just compare baseball's full-windup pitch to football's forward pass—but all throws share muscular movement sequences that speed the object being thrown.

The Major Muscles of the Overhand Throw

The final throwing motion—the delivery—sums up muscular forces generated by a leg and hip thrust, a hip and trunk rotation, a pull-through and rotation of the shoulder, and the wrist and fingers' flex/extension.

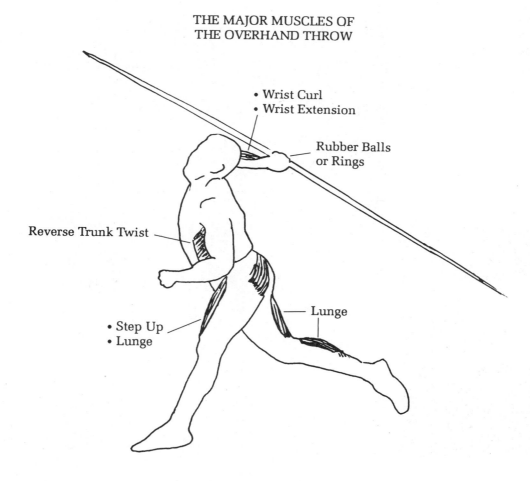

THE MAJOR MUSCLES OF
THE OVERHAND THROW

• Wrist Curl
• Wrist Extension

Rubber Balls
or Rings

Reverse Trunk Twist

Lunge

• Step Up
• Lunge

OVERHAND THROW PROGRAM

* One additional hip and leg thrust movement to that already selected for the Sports Strength Program.

Adults/Late Adolescents

Off-Season: Two or three training days per week, per exercise. Follow the set/rep patterns outlined in the periodization schedule on page 79.

In-Season: Two sets of six repetitions at 80 percent of 1RM, two or three training days per week, per exercise.

Kids/Early Adolescents

First-Year Program: Perform two sets of ten repetitions at 65 percent of 1RM, two days per week throughout the year.

Second-Year Program: Begin a modified off-season periodization schedule as outlined on page 79 after completing the first year of a strength-training program.

Bent-Arm Pullover

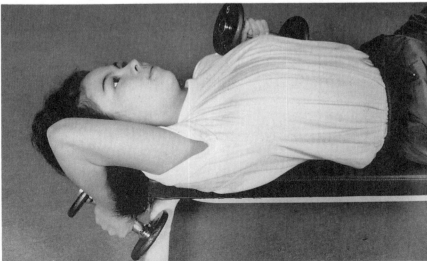

Cable Pulley Overhand Throw

Duplicate your event's specific throwing motion as closely as possible in the strength-building exercise. This makes it more likely that the increased strength can apply to a competition throw. If cables are unavailable, improvise with a dumbbell.

Tricep Extension

Stronger triceps facilitate the arm's final extension during the throw.

Step-up or Lunge

This additional leg-thrust movement emphasizes the importance of legs and hips to a successful throwing motion.

Leg Curl

Including the leg curl for the hamstrings balances the two leg-thrust exercises that primarily strengthen the quads.

Wrist Curl, Wrist Extension, Finger Rings

The throw is a summation of forces beginning at the feet and ending at the final extension of the fingers—the last point of transfer between the muscular force and the object thrown.

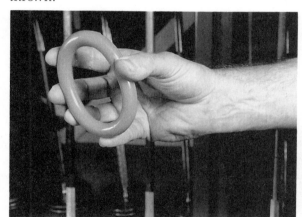

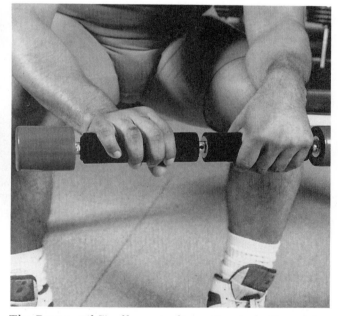

The Power-stik™ offers an alternative to both wrist curls and wrist extension exercises. The manufacturer's address can be found on page 220.

Detailed descriptions and photographs of every exercise recommended in this chapter can be found starting on page 98. Carefully follow those exercise descriptions.

In the next chapter: a strength-training program designed specifically for your sport!

CHAPTER THIRTEEN

TRAINING PROGRAMS FOR YOUR SPORT

ARCHERY

"Your mastery of the muscles involved in an archery shot is complicated by the fact that some muscles are used statically, while others are used dynamically. However, with practice you can blend these various muscle movements into one of the most beautiful physical actions to be seen—the positive, controlled, accurate shooting of an arrow. When you have made that good shot—knowing exactly how you did it—your pleasure and confidence will increase immeasurably.

When working to build *strength and tone*, do not try to develop bulk. Large, bulky muscles, though powerful, may not have the suppleness required to withstand the constant stretching and contracting needed for shot after shot. The bulky muscled person will also have more troubles with string clearance then will a slimmer person."

—John C. Williams, 1972 Olympic gold medal winner and
1984 U.S. Olympic coach

Special note to archers

Drawing the bowstring is a pure sports application of static muscle contraction. Duplicate that static contraction by pulling against an immovable cable pulley or other isometric device.

A clean string-release requires explosive contraction of the muscles that extend the fingers. The pictured hand exercise works those muscles.

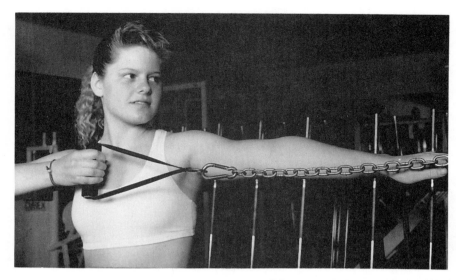

The isometric bow pull duplicates the static contraction inherent in archery. See page 70 for a review of isometric training.

Finger extension exercises, like the isometric finger ring flexion pictured to the right, facilitate string release.

ARCHERY PROGRAM: ALL AGES

Year-round Program: Two sets of ten repetitions per set at 65 percent of 1RM; two training days per week. The exercise array reflects archery's diverse strength requirements while focusing on the upper-body muscles responsible for the pull, hold, and string release.

Page	Exercises	Primary Purpose
165	1. Isometric Bow Pull	Hold string steady
165	2. Hand Ring Extension	String release
114	3. Bent-over Dumbbell Row	Pull
100	4. Lunge	Leg strength
108	5. Bench Press (close grip)	Tricep and shoulder strength
103	6. Sit-up	Torso stabilization
107	7. Stiff-Legged Deadlift	Torso stabilization
130	8. Wrist Curl	String grip
155	9. Hand Ring Flexion	String grip

BASEBALL/SOFTBALL

"The midsection area is the key link between the baseball pitcher's hip musculature and the shoulder girdle. These groups are responsible for efficient transferral of the forces created by the lower-body actions into the upper-body movements, and eventually into the baseball's flight. It is important to note that these areas (abdominals, low back, etc.) need to be trained to develop muscular strength and power, not just muscular endurance. Therefore, these areas should be trained with similar program design as other high-force-producing body parts. That is, these structures should be trained with similar arrangements of training volume (sets, reps), training frequency (sessions/week), and duration."

—Pat Jacobs, associate strength and conditioning coach, University of Miami

Don't make the mistake of swinging several bats or using a donut while warming up in the on-deck circle. Research conclusively proves that the additional weight adversely affects timing and bat velocity at the plate.

Different positions require different physical talents. That's why Nolan Ryan pitched and Willie Mays earned his living as a center fielder.

Strength-training programs also differ by position. A pitcher's workout narrowly focuses on the muscles and movements of the throw, whereas the center fielder demands a broader training agenda to strengthen batting and running.

Most young baseball players need a program that strengthens all muscle groups—increasing batting speed, throwing speed and distance, and the leg speed necessary when running bases or chasing the ball.

Special note to baseball players

Whether hitting or throwing, leg and hip force is transferred through the midsection to the shoulders, arms, and hands, and then applied to the ball or bat. Any weak link will prevent that transfer. The entire body must be strengthened, usually off-season when training time and energy aren't split between the weight room and the playing field.

The suggested general baseball programs, age-grouped with respect to growth and development, strengthen all the positions. Supplementary exercises strengthen batting and throwing.

GENERAL BASEBALL/SOFTBALL PROGRAM
Adults and Late Adolescents

Off-Season Program: Follow the set/rep schedule described in the periodization program found on page 79.

In-Season Program: Two sets of ten repetitions at 65 percent 1RM, two training days per week.

Page	Exercises	Primary Purpose
98	1. Squat	Leg and hip thrust
104	2. Leg Raise	Knee lift/jackknife
107	3. Stiff-Legged Deadlift	Back extension/torso stabilization
140	4. Reverse Trunk Twist	Torso rotation
100	5. Lunge	Leg and hip thrust
111	6. Push Press	Upper-body thrust
116	7. Power Clean	Upper-body pull
143	8. Frog Hop	Leg and hip thrust

GENERAL BASEBALL/SOFTBALL PROGRAM
Kids and Early Adolescents

Year-round Program: Two sets of ten repetitions per set at 65 percent of 1RM, two training days per week. After a year of continuous training, younger athletes can begin a modified off-season periodization schedule as outlined on page 79.

Page	Exercises	Primary Purpose
99	1. Leg Press	Hip and leg thrust
100	2. Lunge	Hip and leg thrust
143	3. Frog Hop	Hip and leg thrust
140	4. Reverse Trunk Twist	Torso rotation
114	5. Bent-over Dumbbell Row	Upper-body pull
108	6. Bench Press (close grip)	Upper-body thrust
107	7. Stiff-Legged Deadlift	Torso stabilization
104	8. Leg Raise	Knee lift/torso stabilization

BATTING

If hitting is your primary strength-training goal, follow your age-specific general baseball program plus the following:

Page	Exercises	Primary Purpose
135	1. Cable Pulley Swing	Event-specific swing
130	2. Wrist Curl	Forearm/wrist/hand strength
131	3. Wrist Extension	Forearm/wrist/hand strength
155	4. Hand Ring Flexion	Bat control/hand strength

OVERHAND THROWING

"The speed (velocity) of a baseball pitch is determined by the muscular forces exerted prior to the release of the ball."

—Pat Jacobs, associate strength and conditioning coach,
University of Miami

If overhand throwing is your strength-training focus, add the following exercises to strengthen and prevent injury in specifically selected throwing muscles.

OVERHAND THROWING

Page	Exercises	Primary Purpose
134	1. Cable Pulley Overhand Throw	Event specific throw
138	2. Rotator Cuff Series	Injury prevention
125	3. Alternating Dumbbell Pullover	Ball pull-through
155	4. Hand Ring Flexion/Extension	Ball control

UNDERHAND PITCHING

Combine elements of the age-specific general baseball program and several specialty exercises, including the underhand cable throw.

Page	Exercises	Primary Purpose
168	1. Cable Pulley Underhand Pitch	Event specific throw
130	2. Wrist Curl	Forearm-wrist action
138	3. Rotator Cuff Series	Injury prevention
155	4. Hand Ring Flexion/Extension	Ball control

In-season strength-training modifications

More time and energy spent on practices and games leaves less for your strength-training program. Hence, in-season strength training's objective is *strength maintenance*. The primary difference in a maintenance program is that training volume is reduced in one of three ways: reducing the number of training days, reducing each exercise's sets while training days remain constant, or reducing both sets and training days. The exact mechanics depend on the team's schedule. I recommend two sets of ten repetitions, twice each week, but the general premise remains: Retain the same array of exercises while balancing weight-room demands against those of on-field training.

Duplicate your normal underhand throwing motion, stepping forward as you pull the cable.

BASKETBALL

"A cursory study of today's athletes and specific athletic events clearly demonstrates that muscular power, strength, and endurance, as well as some degree of muscular hypertrophy, are critical to maximizing athletic potential and reducing athletic injuries. The degree of muscular enhancement is dependent upon the particular sport, individual, and playing position. Basketball as it is played today demands a relatively strong athlete with the agility to effectively use the strength in a coordinated manner."

—Joe Chandler, Lander College, South Carolina

Basketball players are among the most spectacular all-around athletes, and among the strongest. Posting up, jumping, fighting for defensive position, blocking out, and rebounding are obvious examples where strength separates one player from another. Less obvious is that strength impacts every movement—each jump, turn, shot, pass, drive, or block.

Inadequate strength has limited numerous basketball players' development. This is particularly true of younger players, many of whom quit in frustration because physical weakness impedes their skill acquisition.

Greater strength improves all basketball skills; that's true at any age. Stronger passing muscles produce quicker, more accurate passes. Stronger jumping muscles produce higher, quicker jumps. Stronger shooting muscles increase shooting range and accuracy. Put it all together and you have a better basketball player.

BASKETBALL PROGRAM
All Age Groups

Page	Exercises	Primary Purpose
98	1. Squat or Leg Press*	Leg and hip thrust
100	2. Lunge	Leg and hip thrust
143	3. Frog Hop	Leg and hip thrust
127	4. Low-pulley Leg Pull	Knee lift
108	5. Bench-Press (close grip)	Upper-body thrust
113	6. Lat Machine Pull-down	Upper-body pull (close grip)
107	7. Stiff-Legged Deadlift	Back extension
104	8. Leg Raises	Knee lift/torso stabilization
155	9. Hand Ring Flexion	Ball control
122	10. Toe Raise, Leg Press Machine	Ankle extension

* The leg press is the recommended exercise for kids and early adolescents, who should avoid squats until shoulder-girdle and torso strength are adequately developed.

Off-Season Sets and Reps: Adults and late adolescents should follow the set/rep patterns described in the periodization program found on page 79. Younger athletes should follow a year-round program of two days per week, with two sets of ten repetitions per exercise at 65 percent of 1RM, until they have continuously trained for one year. Thereafter, they can begin a modified off-season periodization program.

In-Season Sets and Reps: All athletes perform two sets of ten repetitions at 65 percent of 1RM, two training days per week.

In-Season Programs

Maintaining strength in-season requires continued strength training. Otherwise, much of the off-season gains will be lost.

Since energy and time are limited, the coach and athlete must find a balance between the weight room and the court. The previous chart suggests two sets of ten repetitions per exercise in-season. Older players' in-season training days have been reduced to twice a week—the same frequency suggested year-round for younger players. This further lowering reflects the stresses of in-season demands.

Special note on the jump

The basketball program builds overall strength while focusing on the jump's muscles. Let's take a look at some of them:

The spinal erectors and the hip extensors contract explosively, straightening the back and thrusting the hips forward during the jump. In the gym, those muscles are strengthened by the stiff-legged deadlift and the frog hop, among others.

The thigh and calf are the most obvious muscle groups integral to the jump. The squat, leg press, and lunge strengthen the thighs; the toe raise strengthens the calf. A less-obvious contribution to the jump is the movement of the shoulder girdle and arms. The bench press and pull-down strengthen those muscle groups.

The abdominals—strengthened by the weighted sit-ups—stabilize the torso during the jarring impact of the landing.

Page 143 details depth jumps, a frog hop variation. Depth jumps are an excellent addition to any jumping program, but don't try them until you've done other leg-strengthening exercises for at least a year.

BOWLING

Pick up a sixteen-pound bowling ball and you'll immediately realize the sport's strength requirements. In fact, too little strength is the most common cause of poor bowling technique. The National Bowling Council states that more than 130 muscles are involved in a standard ball delivery—important news for the 19 million bowlers between the ages of five and seventeen who bowl at least once a year.

Bowlers can use their Sports Strength Program to develop the general strength that adds momentum to the ball, as well as practicing elements of the grip program for better control.

BOWLING

All Age Groups

Year-round Program: Adults/late adolescents: three sets of eight repetitions at 75 percent 1RM, two or three days per week. Kids/early adolescents: two sets of ten repetitions at 65 percent of 1RM, two days per week.

Page	Exercises	Primary Purpose
100	1. Lunge	Hip and leg thrust/approach
114	2. Bent-over Dumbbell Row	Upper-body pull
108	3. Bench Press (close grip)	Upper-body thrust
103	4. Sit-up	Torso stabilization during delivery
107	5. Stiff-Legged Deadlift	Torso extension/stabilization
130	6. Wrist Curl	Forearm-wrist strength/ball control
131	7. Wrist Extension	Forearm-wrist strength/ball control
136	8. Dumbbell Biceps Curl	Prevent injuries: elbow and arm

BOXING

"A broad, international, medical consensus that boxing is medically wrong and should be abolished has developed in the last few years ... the British, Canadian, Australian, American, New York State, Californian, and World Medical Associations; the American Academy of Pediatrics; and the American Academy of Neurology have formally stated that boxing is medically wrong and should be abolished."

—George D. Lundberg, M.D., editor, *Journal of the American Medical Association*

"I think amateur boxing is a safe sport. It has suffered the brunt of a highly emotional campaign on the part of the AMA—an emotional path without any good, scientific backing."

—Gerald R. Litel, M.D., Sports Medicine Committee chair, U.S. Amateur Boxing Federation

"I have always adhered to two principles. The first one is to train hard and get into the best possible physical condition. The second is to forget all about the other fellow until you face him in the ring and the bell sounds for the fight."

—Rocky Marciano, heavyweight boxing champion

A generation ago, boxers avoided weight training like the plague, believing that it slowed their movements. But the facts reveal something different: In a study of amateur boxers conducted at the United States Olympic training center, boxers punched faster and harder after only weeks of strength training.

Today, many successful boxers strength-train to increase punching power, muscular endurance, and speed. Evander Holyfield, the world heavyweight champion at the time of this writing, makes strength training an integral part of his total training program.

Reread chapter 1 if you're a boxer or manager with doubts about weight training's contribution toward increasing punching power, and don't underestimate the impact that greater strength has on a fighter's confidence as he steps through the ropes.

Special note to boxers

Leg exercises emphasize leg drive and the importance of hip rotation in powering a punch. The reverse trunk twist and barbell plate twist strengthen upper-body muscles, adding to the punch's rotational force.

Anyone who has boxed appreciates the contribution of strong

hands, forearms, and wrists in delivering a punch and reducing upper-extremity injuries. Hence, hand and forearm exercises are another integral part of the boxer's strength-training program.

The alternate dumbbell bench press is a modified Sports Strength Program upper-body thrust movement; it more closely mimics the "elbows-in" punching motion while allowing a greater range than the regular barbell bench press.

BOXING PROGRAM
Adults and Late Adolescents

Page	Exercises	Primary Purpose
100	1. Lunge	Hip and leg thrust
133	2. Alternate Dumbbell Bench Press	Upper-body thrust: punch
101	3. Step-up	Hip and leg thrust
103	4. Sit-up	Torso rotation
99	5. Leg Press	Hip and leg thrust
130	6. Wrist Curl	Injury prevention
114	7. One-Arm Dumbbell Row*	Upper-body pull: spike or pull-up
131	8. Wrist Extension	Wrist extension
155	9. Hand Ring Flexion	Injury prevention
140	10. Reverse Trunk Twist*	Torso rotation
107	11. Stiff-Legged Deadlift	Back stabilization
165	12. Hand Ring Extension	Injury prevention

* Perform *one-arm dumbbell rows* and *reverse trunk twists* during one workout, *barbell plate twists* and *pull-ups* the next.

Off-Season Training Schedule: Follow the set/rep schedule outlined in the periodization program found on page 79.

In-Season Sets and Reps: In-season is a time for strength maintenance rather than strength building. As bouts draw near, reduce sets and reps to accommodate traditional training's increased demands. Two sets of eight repetitions at 70 percent of 1RM, two days per week, is an appropriate strength-training schedule.

BOXING PROGRAM
Kids and Early Adolescents

Year-round Program: Younger boxers perform two sets of ten repetitions at 65 percent of 1RM, two days per week throughout the year. After a year of continuous strength training, younger athletes can begin a modified off-season periodization schedule as outlined on page 79.

Exercise Selection: Younger boxers perform the same strength-training exercises recommended for adults. However, if exercise volume is too demanding, the athlete and coach should reduce the training regimen to six exercises: lunge, alternate dumbbell bench press, reverse trunk rotation, pull-up, stiff-legged deadlift, and sit-up.

CYCLING

"Strength improves when a muscle is placed at an overload of two-thirds of its maximal strength. Maximal strength gain is best achieved using four to six repetitions and three to four sets for each muscle group. Training should occur three times per week until a point is reached when increases in strength no longer improve performance. At that point a maintenance program should be sufficient. One set of six to eight repetitions for each muscle group is required for maintenance. Most competitive cyclists practice strength training during their off-season, and include a range of upper body exercises in order to promote arm-specific strength gains to supplement force application to the pedals in climbing, acceleration, sprinting, and so on."

—Klaus Klausen, in *Physiology of Sport*

Strength training *won't* help the cyclist avoid bees, widen peripheral vision, or increase oxygen delivery to fatigued muscles during the latter stages of a 100-kilometer road race. But strength training *can* substantially improve the cyclist's pedal power during sprints and climbs, *can* somewhat enhance muscular endurance, and *can* lessen or prevent a broad spectrum of cycling-related injuries.

Pure strength finds its greatest application in athletic performances demanding maximum power and speed generated through each muscular movement over short periods of time—just think of the explosive put of a shot, a football punt, a knockout punch, or a volleyball spike. Cycling provides another example in which improved sports performance is achieved by increasing the athlete's power and speed.

The shorter the race or the steeper the hill, the more muscular strength becomes a factor in ultimate performance. A 200-meter sprint, lasting less than twelve seconds, depends on muscular strength. In a sprint this short, muscular endurance is a relatively minor factor, as is aerobic endurance. When all other physiological and psychological conditions are equal, the stronger cyclist has a significant competitive advantage during short sprints or negotiating a steep hill.

Another of the road racer's needs that strength training can fulfill is injury prevention. A common ailment among cyclists is low back pain, the result of enduring miles of bumps while maintaining potentially stressful posture. Increased torso strength is thought to reduce low back problems by increasing torso stability. Hence the inclusion of torso-strengthening leg raises, reverse trunk twists, and stiff-legged dead lifts in the cyclist's strength-training program.

By supplementing your time on the bike with weight training, you will help increase your short-burst cycling power and prevent some injuries.

CYCLING PROGRAM
Adults and Late Adolescents

Page	Exercises	Primary Purpose
101	1. Step-up	Hip and leg drive
99	2. Leg Press	Hip and leg drive
116	3. Power Cleans	Upper-body pull: sprints and climbs
104	4. Leg Raise	Knee lift: torso stabilization
132	5. Alternate Upright Row	Upper-body pull: sprints and climbs
107	6. Stiff-Legged Deadlift	Torso stabilization/injury prevention
110	7. Dip	Triceps-shoulder development
128	8. Leg Curl	Knee lift
140	9. Reverse Trunk Twist	Rotational strength
127	10. Cable Pulley Leg Pull	Knee lift

Off-Season Program: Off-season is time for strength building, meaning more sets and greater training frequency. Follow the set/rep schedule outlined in the periodization program found on page 79.

In-Season Sets and Reps: In-season is a time for strength maintenance. Sets and reps are reduced to accommodate the increased demands of road or track work. Two sets of eight repetitions at 70 percent of 1RM, two days per week, is an appropriate schedule.

CYCLING PROGRAM
Kids and Early Adolescents

Page	Exercises	Primary Purpose
101	1. Step-up	Hip and leg drive
99	2. Leg Press	Hip and leg drive
132	3. Alternate Upright Row	Upper-body pull: sprints and climbs
104	4. Leg Raise	Knee lift/torso strength
107	5. Stiff-Legged Deadlift	Torso stabilization; injury prevention
108	6. Bench Press	Triceps and shoulder strength
128	7. Leg Curl	Knee lift: Injury prevention
140	8. Reverse Trunk Twist	Rotational strength

Year-round Program: Perform two sets of ten repetitions at 65 percent of 1RM, two days per week throughout the first training year. Thereafter, begin a modified off-season periodization program as outlined on page 79.

FENCING

"Leg strength is essential in fencing. Some exercises which will assist in the development of leg muscles are various types of knee bends. . . . Although there is some controversy of some deep knee bends because of the possible damage to the knee joint, most of the authors who have written on conditioning programs for fencers have included this type of exercise. Since the knee is in the bent position in many of the techniques, this can be a beneficial exercise if done correctly."

—Yvonne Dempsey, State University College, New Paltz, New York

Imagine the ease and speed of executing a lunge—the most important offensive movement in fencing—if your legs were 200 percent stronger. It can happen through strength training.

Leg strength doesn't act alone. The lunge demands synchronous contractions from hundreds of muscles, including thumb and forefinger to manipulate the pommel; shoulder and arm muscles to extend the foil; and abdominal and back muscles to stabilize the torso.

The fencer's program builds overall movement strength while emphasizing the elements—shoulders, grip, and legs—that have the greatest impact.

FENCING PROGRAM
Adults and Late Adolescents

Off-Season Program: Two or three training days per week, per exercise. Follow the set/rep patterns outlined in the periodization schedule on page 79.

In-Season Sets and Reps: Two sets of eight repetitions at 75 percent of 1RM, two or three training days per week, per exercise.

Page	Exercises	Primary Purpose
100	1. Lunge	Hip and leg thrust: event specific
101	2. Step-up	Hip and leg thrust
104	3. Leg Raise	Knee lift/torso stabilization
127	4. Low-pulley Leg Pull	Knee lift
108	5. Bench-Press (close grip)	Upper-body thrust/foil thrust
107	6. Stiff-Legged Deadlift	Torso stabilization
132	7. Alternate Upright Row	Upper-body pull: shoulder strength
130	8. Wrist Curl	Grip; foil control
131	9. Wrist Extension	Foil control
155	10. Hand Ring Flexion*	Hand strength; foil control

* Emphasize thumb-index pinch.

FENCING PROGRAM

Kids and Early Adolescents

Year-round Program: Perform two sets of ten repetitions at 65 percent of 1RM, two days per week throughout the year. Begin a modified off-season periodization schedule as outlined on page 79, after completing the first year of a strength-training program.

Exercise Selection: Perform the same strength-training exercises recommended for adults. However, if exercise volume is too demanding, reduce the regimen to five exercises: lunge, bench press, stiff-legged deadlift, alternate upright row, and leg raise.

FOOTBALL

"Football is football. The best high school players usually make the best college players. The best college players usually make the best pro players. It's just that the cream gets a little thinner as you go along."

—Ken Sims, New England Patriots

"When I graduated from high school, I weighed only 190 pounds, and therefore was not recruited by any colleges. I began to lift weights before going to a small college, and added weight throughout my early college athletic career. I transferred to Minnesota, where I continued to lift, and gained not only strength but speed. While at Minnesota, my body weight increased to 230 pounds, and I power-cleaned 350 pounds from the hang above my knees.

"At Minnesota we did a lot of Olympic movements with the weights, and now, at Denver, we also do a lot of Olympic lifting. I feel that this has continually increased my ability as a player, and that our lifting program transfers to the on-field performance."

—Karl Mecklenburg, Denver Broncos lineman

Special note to football players

Football and strength training go hand in hand. In fact, the average Division I college football player has lifted weights for six years before he enters college.

The Sports Strength Program is a basic strength builder that benefits all players—kickers to 300-pound linemen. The added exercises reflect the different positions' strength needs.

LINEMAN PROGRAM
Adults and Late Adolescents

Page	Exercises	Primary Purpose
98	1. Squat	Hip and leg thrust
102	2. Hack Machine*	Hip and leg thrust
116	3. Power Clean	Upper-body pull
111	4. Push Press	Upper-body thrust
107	5. Stiff-Legged Deadlift	Back extension
103	6. Sit-up	Jackknife
140	7. Reverse Trunk Twist	Torso rotation

* Substitute the lunge for the hack squat if the athlete's shoulders are too narrow or not strong enough to accommodate the machine.

Off-Season: Two or three training days per week per exercise. Follow the set/rep patterns outlined in the periodization schedule on page 79.

In-Season Sets and Reps: Two sets of six repetitions at 80 percent of 1RM, two or three training days per week per exercise.

LINEMAN PROGRAM

Kids and Early Adolescents

Page	Exercises	Primary Purpose
99	1. Leg Press	Hip and leg thrust
102	2. Hack Machine*	Hip and leg thrust
115	3. Seated Cable Long Pull	Upper-body pull
108	4. Bench Press	Upper-body thrust
107	5. Stiff-Legged Deadlift	Back extension
103	6. Sit-up	Jackknife
140	7. Reverse Trunk Twist	Torso rotation

* Substitute the lunge for the hack squat if the athlete's shoulders are too narrow or not strong enough to accommodate the machine.

First Year Program: Perform two sets of ten repetitions at 65 percent of 1RM, two days per week throughout the year.

Second Year Program: Begin a modified off-season periodization schedule as outlined on page 79 after completing the first year of strength training.

PUNTERS AND KICKERS PROGRAM

Follow the age-specific program recommended for linemen including exercise selection and appropriate training schedules. Then add the following exercises:

Page	Exercises	Primary Purpose
129	1. Knee Extension	Event-specific movement
127	2. Low-pulley Leg Pull	Knee lift
128	3. Leg Curl	Injury prevention

CENTER: LONG SNAP PROGRAM

Follow the age-specific program recommended for linemen, including exercise selection and appropriate training schedules. Then add the following exercises:

Page	Exercises	Primary Purpose
125	1. Bent-arm Pullover	Ball pull-through
137	2. Tricep Extension	Elbow extension
130	3. Wrist Curl	Forearm-wrist strength
155	4. Hand Ring Flex	Ball control

QUARTERBACK PROGRAM

Quarterbacks should follow the age-specific program recommended for linemen, including exercise selection and appropriate training schedules. To those recommendations, add the following exercises:

Page	Exercises	Primary Purpose
134	1. Cable Pulley Throw	Event-specific movement
137	2. Tricep Extension	Elbow extension
130	3. Wrist Curl	Forearm-wrist strength
155	4. Hand Ring Flex/Extension	Ball control
127	5. Cable Leg Pull	Knee lift
138	6. Rotator Cuff Series	Injury prevention: shoulders
128	7. Leg Curl	Injury prevention: hamstrings

RUNNING BACK/DEFENSIVE BACK/LINEBACKER PROGRAM

Follow the age-specific program recommended for linemen, including exercise selection and appropriate training schedules. To those recommendations, add the following exercises:

Page	Exercises	Primary Purpose
127	1. Cable Leg Pull	Knee lift
128	2. Leg Curl	Injury prevention
100	3. Lunge	Leg and hip thrust
141	4. Barbell Plate Twist	Torso rotation

GOLF

"Don't be fooled when you see a few golfers with potbellies on TV. Most of the PGA Tour players are pretty fair athletes with a high degree of strength and flexibility related to their sport."

—Dr. Gary Wren, master teacher, PGA professional

Every golfer appreciates Dr. Wren's comment; a long drive demands more than swing technique and flight trajectory. All else being equal, the golfer's strength determines the club head's speed, which determines the ball's initial speed as it leaves the tee. This determines how far the ball travels down the fairway. The average golfer achieves an initial ball speed of approximately 125 mph. A long-driving professional can achieve a ball speed exceeding 170 mph.

A full golf swing requires the synchronous movements of hundreds of muscles. From the fingers to the toes, most of the body's muscles contribute to the speed or control of the swing. That's an indication that the golfer needs a full-body strength-training program—with several exceptions. The golfer should avoid exercises that develop the chest, as that can interfere with a full swing's technical precision. The recommended program emphasizes the grip and forearm—the foundation of an accurate and fast swing.

GOLF PROGRAM
Adults and Late Adolescents

Off-Season Program: Two or three training days per week, per exercise. Follow the set/rep patterns outlined in the periodization schedule on page 79.
In-Season Program: Two sets of eight repetitions at 75 percent of 1RM, two days per week, per exercise.

Page	Exercises	Primary Purpose
100	1. Lunge	Hip and leg thrust
101	2. Step-up	Hip and leg thrust
141	3. Barbell Plate Twist	Torso rotation and stabilization
135	4. Cable Pulley Swing	Event-specific movement
132	5. Alternate Upright Row	Emphasizes shoulder development
107	6. Stiff-Legged Deadlift	Back extension/torso stabilization
130	7. Wrist Curl	Wrist-forearm
131	8. Wrist Extension	Wrist-forearm
155	9. Hand Ring Flexion	Finger-hand strength
112	10. Pull-up	Upper-body pull
103	11. Sit-up	Torso stabilization

GOLF PROGRAM
Kids and Early Adolescents

Year-round Program: Perform two sets of ten repetitions at 65 percent of 1RM, two days per week throughout the year. After completing the first year of a strength-training program, follow a modified off-season periodization schedule as outlined on page 79.

Exercise Selection: Perform the same strength-training exercises recommended for adults. However, if exercise volume is too demanding, reduce the regimen to six exercises: lunge, pull-up, stiff-legged deadlift, alternate upright row, reverse trunk twist, and cable pulley swing.

MARTIAL ARTS

Competitive athletes have benefited from martial arts training. Former All-Pro Dallas tackle Randy White was able to apply the bilateral training inherent in martial arts kicks, punches, and reaction techniques to his ability on the football field.

"The primary consideration for martial artists when weight-training should be to make all of the major muscular structures as genetically strong as possible—without discrimination. Every single muscle group in our bodies has a function in given combat techniques, period.

"Without the proper balance of strength between opposing muscle groups, overall strength in each and every combat technique is diminished."

—Scott Wong, *jow ga* teacher, New York City

"Traditionally, martial artists have done exercises like push-ups and bench presses to build punching power. Appropriate weight-lifting programs are invaluable for proper development, and they can even minimize injuries. In fact, weight lifting can greatly benefit each and every martial artist, building strength and enhancing confidence."

—Mark McGuire, martial arts instructor and former World Karate Association champion

MARTIAL ARTS PROGRAM
Adults/Late Adolescents

Page	Exercises	Primary Purpose
141	1. Barbell Plate Twist	Rotational force
102	2. Hack Machine	Hip and leg thrust
116	3. Power Clean	Upper-body pull
111	4. Push Press	Upper-body thrust
107	5. Stiff-Legged Deadlift	Back extension
103	6. Sit-up	Jackknife
140	7. Reverse Trunk Twist	Torso rotation
98	8. Squat	Hip and leg thrust

Off-Season Program: Two or three training days per week, per exercise. Follow the set/rep patterns outlined in the periodization schedule on page 79.
In-Season Program: Two sets of six repetitions at 80 percent of 1RM, two or three training days per week, per exercise.

MARTIAL ARTS PROGRAM
Kids/Early Adolescents

Page	Exercises	Primary Purpose
141	1. Barbell Plate Twist	Rotational force
102	2. Hack Machine*	Hip and leg thrust
115	3. Seated Cable Long Pull	Upper-body pull
108	4. Bench Press	Upper-body thrust
107	5. Stiff-Legged Deadlift	Back extension
103	6. Sit-up	Jackknife
140	7. Reverse Trunk Twist	Torso rotation
99	8. Leg Press	Hip and leg thrust

* Substitute the lunge for the hack squat if the athlete's shoulders are too narrow or not strong enough to accommodate the machine.

First-Year Program: Perform two sets of ten repetitions at 65 percent of 1RM, two days per week, throughout the year.
Second-Year Program: Begin a modified off-season periodization schedule as outlined on page 79 after completing the first year of a strength-training program.

RACQUETBALL AND SQUASH

Racquetball and squash are quite different games, but each encompasses a group of similar movements and strength demands.

Let's begin with the swing's common components: The swing's force begins with leg drive, is enhanced through hip and torso rotation, and is finally delivered to the ball through the shoulder girdle, arm, and hand muscles. At the hand, the player's objective is to transfer the full force of the body to the racquet, and subsequently the ball. How well this occurs depends on the athlete's grip. Consequently, exercises that develop hand, wrist, and forearm strength are vital.

The Sports Strength Program exercises muscles from toe to hand; to that, add leg-strengthening exercises that reflect the lunging, backpedaling, and lateral movements involved with racquet sports.

RACQUETBALL/SQUASH PROGRAM

Year-round Program: Adults/late adolescents: Three sets of eight repetitions at 75 percent of 1RM; two or three training days per exercise per week. Kids/early adolescents: two sets of ten repetitions at 70 percent of 1RM, two days per week.

Page	Exercises	Primary Purpose
100	1. Lunge	Hip and leg thrust
128	2. Leg Curl	Injury prevention
101	3. Step-up	Hip and leg thrust
140	4. Reverse Trunk Twist	Torso rotation
108	5. Bench Press	Upper-body thrust
114	6. Bent-over Dumbbell Row	Upper-body pull
107	7. Stiff-Legged Deadlift	Back extension
130	8. Wrist Curl	Grip: forearm and wrist strength
131	9. Wrist Extension	Grip: forearm and wrist strength
104	10. Leg Raises	Knee lift/torso stabilization
155	11. Hand Ring, Flex	Racquet manipulation/grip

ROWING

"Some of the earliest rowers, the Athenians and Persians, didn't get quite as much enjoyment out of rowing and probably questioned its health benefits. They rowed to exhaustion in life-or-death battles against each other. Despite being outnumbered, the Athenians usually outrowed their foes. Paintings on ancient pottery revealed that the Athenians rowed on movable slides, while the Persians sat on fixed seats. The sliding seat enables the oarsman to use his entire body in driving the oars, while the fixed seat forces the rower to use arms only."

—Susan Lezotte, writer for *American Rowing*, the official
magazine of the U.S. Rowing Association

The best rowers are the strongest rowers. That's a fact that numerous studies and championship events have validated. Compared to the competition, champion rowers have stronger arms, backs, legs, and hands.

Dry-land training for rowers encompasses training for strength, muscular endurance, and aerobic endurance—three elements indispensable to rowers. Rowing machines are best for developing muscular endurance and, to a lesser degree, aerobic training, but nothing exceeds the standard exercises listed below for building the rower's strength.

The sum strength of your legs, hips, back, and arms supplies most of the stroke drive's force—legs and hips supply the initial 75 percent of the power, the back and arms provide the last 25 percent.

ROWING PROGRAM
Adults and Late Adolescents

Page	Exercises	Primary Purpose
98	1. Squat	Hip and leg thrust
99	2. Leg Press	Hip and leg thrust
116	3. Power Clean	Upper-body pull
111	4. Push Press	Upper-body thrust
107	5. Stiff-Legged Deadlift	Back extension
103	6. Sit-up	Jackknife
118	7. High Pull	Upper-body pull
115	8. Seated Cable Long Pull	Upper-body pull
117	9. Dead Lift	Pulling Power

Note: Why no specific grip exercises? The rower's hands are statically contracted throughout the competition. Just holding the bar during the pulls, rows, and deadlifts trains the hands for static contractions.

Off-Season Program: Two or three training days per week per exercise. Follow the set/rep patterns outlined in the periodization schedule on page 79.

In-Season Program: Two sets of six repetitions at 80 percent of 1RM, two or three training days per week per exercise.

ROWING PROGRAM
Kids and Early Adolescents

Page	Exercises	Primary Purpose
99	1. Leg Press	Hip and leg thrust
101	2. Step-up	Hip and leg thrust
115	3. Seated Cable Long Pull	Upper-body pull
108	4. Bench Press	Upper-body thrust
107	5. Stiff-Legged Deadlift	Back extension
103	6. Sit-Up	Jackknife
114	7. Bent-over dumbbell Row	Upper-body pull
115	8. Seated Cable Long Pull	Upper-body pull
117	9. Deadlift	Pulling power

Note: Why no specific grip exercises? The rower's hands are statically contracted throughout the competition. Holding the bar during the pulls, rows, and deadlifts trains the hands sufficiently for static contractions.

First-Year Program: Perform two sets of ten repetitions at 65 percent of 1RM, two days per week throughout the year.

Second-Year Program: Begin a modified off-season periodization schedule as outlined on page 79 after completing the first year of strength training.

NORDIC SKIING

"Nordic ski racing is considered to be one of the most physically demanding sports. Both the 15- and 30-kilometer events raced over undulating, snow-packed and often icy courses offer a true test of an athlete's physical strength and stamina as well as mental toughness. Nordic skiers are characteristically low in body fat, have high VO_2 max values, and possess explosive strength. . . . Nordic ski racing is an intense power/endurance sport requiring superior cardiovascular fitness together with muscular strength. But the importance of strength to the Nordic skier is primarily due to its role in power production. Power is essential in skiing or skating uphill, and going all-out on the downhill and the flat."

—Patrick O'Shea, Ed.D.

Nordic, or cross-country, skiing requires a marathoner's stamina and a decathlete's overall body strength. That's one reason exercise machines duplicating cross-country skiing motions have captured the public's fancy.

The Nordic skiers' recommended program combines the Sports Strength Program's overall strength-building multijoint exercises with exercises that mimic poling action and the hip flexion that lifts the ski forward.

NORDIC SKIING PROGRAM
Adults and Late Adolescents

Page	Exercises	Primary Purpose
98	1. Squat	Hip and leg thrust
99	2. Leg Press	Hip and leg thrust
116	3. Power Clean	Upper-body pull
108	4. Bench Press	Upper-body thrust
105	5. Back Extension	Back extension
103	6. Sit-up	Jackknife
100	7. Lunge	Hip and leg thrust
115	8. Seated Cable Long Pull	Upper-body pull
128	9. Leg Curl	Injury prevention
130	10. Wrist Curl	Forearm strength
131	11. Wrist Extension	Forearm strength

Off-Season Program: Two or three training days per week per exercise. Follow the set/rep patterns outlined in the periodization schedule on page 79.

Off-Season Program: In-Season: Two sets of six repetitions at 80 percent of 1RM, two or three training days per week per exercise.

NORDIC SKIING PROGRAM
Kids and Early Adolescents

Page	Exercises	Primary Purpose
98	1. Leg Press	Hip and leg thrust
101	2. Step-up	Hip and leg thrust
115	3. Seated Cable Long Pull	Upper-body pull
108	4. Bench Press (close grip)	Upper-body thrust
105	5. Back Extension	Back extension
103	6. Sit-up	Jackknife
100	7. Lunge	Hip and leg thrust
114	8. Bent-over Dumbbell Row	Upper-body pull
128	9. Leg Curl	Injury prevention
130	10. Wrist Curl	Forearm strength
131	11. Wrist Extension	Forearm strength

First-Year Program: Perform two sets of ten repetitions at 65 percent of 1RM, two days per week throughout the year.

Second-Year Program: Begin a modified off-season periodization schedule as outlined on page 79 after completing the first year of a strength-training program.

SOCCER

"The rules are very simple. Basically it's this: If it moves, kick it; if it doesn't move, kick it until it does."

—Phil Woosnam, North American Soccer League commissioner

At first glance, soccer depends exclusively on the lower back, abdominals, hip, and leg muscles. But soccer is a full-body game that demands a full-body program. For example, throws and head balls can be improved by strengthening upper-body muscle groups.

At the elite level, the player's position somewhat determines the content of the strength-training program. Strikers and stoppers might emphasize exercises that aid in jumping and neck balls; wings, midfielders, and fullbacks might spend the most time improving leg strength and muscular endurance. But at the high school level, the coach should advocate a full-body program without specialization, allowing for the greatest possible interchange of players.

The recommended program for soccer emphasizes leg exercises but includes several upper-body exercises. No need for a program to strengthen the grip—there's nothing to hold.

SOCCER PROGRAM
Adults and Late Adolescents

Page	Exercises	Primary Purpose
98	1. Squats	Leg and hip thrust
100	2. Lunge	Leg and hip thrust
112	3. Pull-ups	Upper-body pull
128	4. Leg Curl	Prevent hamstring injury
107	5. Stiff-Legged Deadlift	Back extension
111	6. Push Press	Upper-body thrust
140	7. Reverse Trunk Twist	Rotational strength/torso stabilization
104	8. Leg Raises	Knee lift/kick/torso stabilization

Off-Season Program: Follow the set/rep patterns described in the periodization program found on page 79.
In-Season Program: Two sets of ten repetitions at 65 percent 1RM, two training days per week.

SOCCER PROGRAM
Kids and Early Adolescents

Page	Exercises	Primary Purpose
101	1. Step-ups	Hip and leg thrust
100	2. Lunge	Hip and leg thrust
112	3. Pull-ups	Upper-body pull
105	4. Back Extension	Back extension/torso stabilization
140	5. Reverse Trunk Twist	Torso rotation/torso stabilization
104	6. Leg Raises	Knee lift/kick/torso stabilization
108	7. Bench Press	Upper-body thrust

Year-round Program: Two sets of ten repetitions per set at 65 percent of 1RM; two training days per week. After a year of steady training, younger athletes can begin a modified off-season periodization schedule as outlined on page 79.

SWIMMING

Good swimmers are strong. As the swimmer's muscles strengthen, power increases, propelling the body more quickly through the water.

A sprint stroke summons five times the available strength of each distance stroke, but the value of strength training is universal. Both strength-trained sprinters and distance swimmers have more power available for each stroke, resulting in faster times.

OFF-SEASON SWIMMING PROGRAM
All Age Groups

Page	Exercises	Primary Purpose
99	1. Leg Press (single leg)	Hip and leg thrust
100	2. Lunge	Hip and leg thrust
128	3. Leg Curl	Knee flexion: breaststroke
103	4. Sit-up	Torso stabilization
124	5. Dumbbell Bench Fly	Pectoral development
127	6. Cable Pulley Leg Pull	Knee lift: breaststroke
115	7. Seated Cable Long Pull	Upper-body pull: all strokes
105	8. Back Extension	Stabilization: injury prevention
112	9. Pull-up	Upper-body pull: all strokes
132	10. Alternate Upright Row	Upper-body pull
193	11. Swim Machine or Cables	Stroke-specific strength
138	12. Rotator Cuff Series	Injury prevention

Adults/Late Adolescents

Two or three training days per week per exercise. Follow the set/rep patterns outlined in the periodization schedule on page 79.

Kids/Early Adolescents

First-Year Program: Perform two sets of ten repetitions at 65 percent of 1RM, two days per week throughout the year.

Second-Year Program: Begin a modified off-season periodization schedule as outlined on page 79 after completing the first year of a strength-training program.

IN-SEASON SWIMMING PROGRAM
All Ages

Page	Exercises	Primary Purpose
193	1. Swim Machine or Cables	Event-specific strength
103	2. Sit-up	Torso stabilization: injury prevention
105	3. Back Extension	Torso stabilization: injury prevention
138	4. Rotator Cuff Series	Injury prevention

Adults/Late Adolescents

Two sets of six repetitions at 80 percent of 1RM, two or three training days per week per exercise.

Kids/Early Adolescents

Two sets of six repetitions at 80 percent of 1RM, two training days per week per exercise.

In-Season Training Brevity

The brevity of the in-season strength-training program reflects the rigorous physical demands encountered by the average swimmer. As a result, weight-room exercises focus on injury prevention and event-specific strength maintenance. Over the course of the season, the swimmer will experience an absolute strength loss in some muscle groups, but the strength/power output specific to the biomechanics and rate of the competitive stroke is retained.

Training-Specific Strokes

The best dry-land exercises most closely duplicate the swimming stroke. Of equipment commonly found in weight rooms, pulleys and benches are the most effective in duplicating the biomechanics of a swimmer's stroke in piecemeal fashion: leg stroke is duplicated during one exercise, the shoulder girdle stroke during another.

Dry-land training machines designed specifically for swimmers are best at mimicking a swimmer's motion in the water, however. One such machine is pictured below.

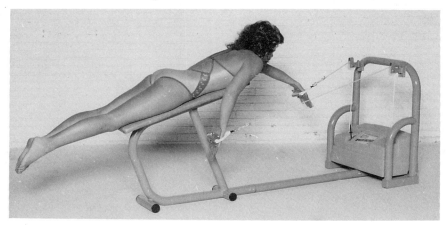

Include pulleys or a swim-machine in your resistance-training program every workout. Duplicate your competitive stroke the best that you can.

Strength Training to Prevent Injuries

Shoulder injuries

Since the shoulder girdle produces the primary propulsive force of any stroke, it's no surprise that the most frequently reported swimming injuries occur at the shoulder joint. This is particularly true for the free-style and backstroke because of their complete shoulder rotation.

Strength-training the shoulders in the off-season helps prevent in-season injuries. That's why the off-season program is loaded with specific shoulder exercises: the rotator cuff series, upright row, and, to a lesser degree, the pull-up, dumbbell fly, and long pull.

Lower-back injuries

The butterfly's numerous, explosive kicks produce a relatively high incidence of lower back problems. By strengthening and stabilizing the torso, the back extension and the weighted sit-up help prevent lower-back injuries; for that reason, they are included in both the off-season and in-season programs.

TENNIS

"Before initiating a training program for a skilled tennis player, it is important to remember that tennis is a whole-body sport and, in fact, the majority of force generated in an aggressive tennis stroke comes from the ground and larger body parts. For this reason, it should be assumed that tennis is a lower-body sport as much, if not more, than it is an upper-body sport. It is also important to bear in mind that tennis is a game of quick actions, agility, and power. For this reason, strength workouts must be combined with power and quickness workouts. Muscular strength and endurance should be developed for the generation and accommodation of force in the calf, quadriceps, hamstrings, abdominals, lower back, pectoral muscles, deltoids, and muscles of the upper limb."

—Jack Groppel, University of Illinois at Urbana-Champaign, Departments of Physical Education and of Bioengineering

TENNIS PROGRAM
All Ages

Page	Exercises	Primary Purpose
100	1. Lunge	Hip and leg thrust
99	2. Leg Press	Hip and leg thrust
127	3. Cable Pulley Leg Pull	Knee lift: first step
140	4. Reverse Trunk Twist	Rotational force
103	5. Sit-up	Torso stabilization/rotation
105	6. Back Extensions	Torso stabilization/rotation
108	7. Bench Press	Upper-body thrust
135	8. Cable Pulley Swing	Stroke-specific strength
114	9. Bent-Over Dumbbell Row	Upper-body pull
130	10. Wrist Curl	Racket control: force transfer to rack.
131	11. Wrist Extension	Racket control: force trans. to racket
132	12. Alternate Upright Row	Upper-body pull

Adults/Late Adolescents

Off-Season Program: Two or three training days per week per exercise. Follow the set/rep patterns outlined in the periodization schedule on page 79.
In-Season Program: Two sets of six repetitions at 80 percent of 1RM, two or three training days per week per exercise.

Kids/Early Adolescents

First-Year Program: Perform two sets of ten repetitions at 65 percent of 1RM, two days per week throughout the year.
Second-Year Program: Begin a modified off-season periodization schedule as outlined on page 79 after completing the first year of a strength-training program.

TRACK AND FIELD

The strength demands of track and field are as varied as the events. Consequently, no one program can best serve all track-and-field athletes.

We'll explore the specific strength requirements and appropriate strength programs of the throws, the jumps, pole vault, sprints and hurdles, and distance events. Let's begin with the throws: shot put, discus, and javelin.

The Throws

Strength training is crucial to the throwing events, but brute force isn't enough. The program must attack the specific muscles that directly impact the throwing movement.

As Patrick O'Shea notes in the Fall 1991 issue of *Track and Field Quarterly*, "When you select your training exercises, remember the concept of specificity, which is the duplication of a skill as closely as possible in terms of muscle groups, range of motion, and speed of movement."

The strength-building programs suggested later in this section combine general strength-building exercises and specialized exercises specific to the individual throwing movements.

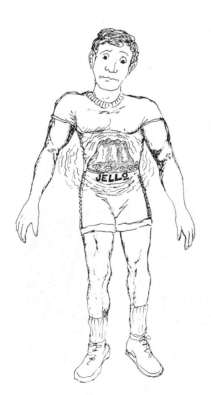

Special note to throwers

The fingers are the last link in a chain of muscular force that begins at the foot, travels the length of the body, and transfers the summated forces to the shot, discus, or javelin. But don't assume that the hands and fingers are adequately strengthened by gripping a barbell during the Sports Strength Program. Throws demand dynamic contractions. That's the reason the recommended programs include *dynamic* exercises to strengthen the fingers and hands.

Abdominal Strength

The midsection is the only path through which the leg drive's force can reach the upper body. Optimal transference requires a midsection strong enough to transfer that force. That being the case, it makes sense to strength-train the abdominals using the same principles and concepts applicable to any other muscle group—low reps and heavy weights.

Use progressive resistance when training the midsection. Don't fall into the trap of high-repetition sets of abdominal work—high reps develop muscular endurance, not muscular strength!

THE SHOT PUT

"One of the major keys to shot-putting using any style is basic leg strength. In considering weight-training workouts, a balance of 80 to 85 percent of the work should be for the legs, with the remainder going to the upper body."

—Don Lukens, Loy Norrix High School, Kalamazoo, Michigan

I believe that three lifts—the parallel squat, push press, and bench press—must be included in any weight-training program for shot putters."

—Mark Erickson, assistant track coach, California State University, Stanislaus

Specificity applied Training with a Heavy Shot

Many athletes succeed with a heavy training implement. For example, the athlete throwing a twelve-pound shot in competition trains with a sixteen-pound shot. This conforms to two aspects of the specificity principle: The resistance training affects the same muscle groups as those called upon during competition, and the movement is identical (or nearly so) to the competition movement.

Speed, the third aspect of the principle of specificity, is somewhat slower when using a heavy implement. That's expected, which is why heavy implements are an off-season or early-season training tool. As the competitive season progresses, most athletes and coaches decrease heavy-implement training to perfect timing.

Single-Leg Press

The single-leg press applies particularly to competitors who use the glide (O'Brien) technique. The exercise more closely duplicates the coordinated muscular demands of the glide technique than do traditional squats and leg presses.

A caveat: perform the exercise for each leg, not just for your drive leg; maintaining bilateral muscular development is important.

THE DISCUS THROW

"Weight training has improved my release explosion, and the length of my throw. I'm looking forward to throwing farther and farther as I become stronger and stronger."

—Kiza Brunner, 1990 National Junior Olympic champion,
Young Women's division

Specificity applied
Chest Fly

The chest fly is more effective than the bench press at duplicating the discus throw's stresses. Pay close attention to the dumbbell or cable's angle.

Discus Stretch Fly

Good form requires that the discus be held well back during the spin, the shoulder and chest pulling only after the thrower has reached the front of the circle. The discus stretch fly mimics the force at the "well back" position.

Hand Strength

Include exercises specific to the hand stress encountered during the discus throw. In practice, that requires using the opposite hand for resistance, or devising a band arrangement as illustrated.

THE JAVELIN THROW

Begin with the dumbbell hanging from the throwing arm. Duplicating your normal throwing motion, lift the dumbbell upward while jack-knifing your torso off the bench. Return to the starting position.

Specificity applied: The Atwood Lift

The Atwood lift was invented by Duncan Atwood, a 1984 Olympic javelin thrower.

Cable Pulls

The concept of the cable pull is analogous to the Atwood lift except that elbow extension is included. Note the grip—it is important to mimic the movement as closely as possible.

THROWS PROGRAM
Adults and Late Adolescents

Page	Exercises	Primary Purpose
98	1. Squat	Leg and hip thrust
99	2. Leg Press	Leg and hip thrust
103	3. Sit-ups	Jackknife
140	4. Reverse Trunk Twist	Torso rotation
107	5. Stiff-Legged Deadlift	Back extension
128	6. Leg Curl*	Hip thrust
116	7. Power Clean	Overall power
118	8. Barbell High Pull	Overall power
108	9. Bench Press	Upper-body thrust
141	10. Barbell Torso Twist	Torso rotation
130	11. Wrist Curl	Hand-forearm
155	12. Hand Rings	Hand-fingers
	13. Specialty Exercise†	

Notes:
* The leg curl is included to balance leg development between the quadriceps and leg biceps.
† Specialty exercises are throw-specific: the Atwood lift or cable pull for a javelin thrower; the discus stretch fly for a discus thrower. Explanations of throw-specific exercises are found in this chapter.

Off-Season Program: Experiment with the periodization program described in chapter 8.

In-Season Program: The thrower continues to build strength during the competitive season, peaking in strength at the year's most important competition. Hence, it is advisable to continue the periodization schedule outlined in chapter 8.

The only time the strength-training program's intensity is reduced is the week of a major competition.

Plyometrics: Many throwers incorporate plyometric exercises into a generalized strength-training program. Depth jumps and frog hops are most frequently recommended. Directions can be found on page 143.

THROWS PROGRAM
Kids and Early Adolescents

Page	Exercises	Primary Purpose
99	1. Leg Press	Hip and leg thrust
101	2. Step-ups	Hip and leg thrust
103	3. Sit-ups	Stabilization
140	4. Reverse Trunk Twist	Torso rotation
105	5. Back Extension	Back extension
115	6. Seated Cable Pull	Upper-body pull
108	7. Bench Press	Upper-body thrust
130	8. Wrist Curl	Hand-forearm
155	9. Hand Rings	Hands-fingers
	10. Specialty Exercise*	

* Specialty exercises are throw-specific: the Atwood lift or cable pull for a javelin thrower; the discus stretch fly for a discus thrower. Explanations of throw-specific exercises are found in this chapter.

Year-round Program: Beginners maintain a constant two sets of ten repetitions, twice each week, throughout the year. After a year of steady training, a strength-training specialist can individually prescribe a modified periodization program consistent with the child's maturation.

THE JUMPS

Special note to jumpers

Excess body weight—including muscular bulk in the upper back, shoulders, and chest—works against gravity. Therefore, the aspiring jumper must be selective. A gain in muscular body weight should be accompanied by significantly more leg, hip, and midsection strength.

Specificity applied
Partial Squat or Leg Press

Partial-movement exercises violate the idea that exercises should move the joint through a full range of motion. But many jump coaches feel that the advantages of a partial squat or leg press outweigh the negatives.

The force experienced by the jumper's partially bent "plant leg" during takeoff far exceeds that of a full-movement squat or leg press. Since the athlete can lift heavier weights performing partial movements at reduced joint angles, takeoff force can be duplicated more closely with partial-movement exercises. In addition, the increased strength reduces the potential for injury by increasing joint stability and the muscle's tension capacity during the high-force takeoff.

High-knee-action hip flexors

The hip flexors (iliopsoas, rectus femoris, pectineus) initiate the high knee action of a jumper's takeoff. Every jumper (and sprinter) should include an exercise specifically for the hip flexors. The following illustrations offer several suggestions.

Special note on abdominal exercises

The jumper's workout must include set/rep patterns that emphasize abdominal strength rather than abdominal endurance. All jumps are explosive events, so don't waste your time with high-repetition, endurance-building sets.

JUMPER'S PROGRAM

Page	Exercises
98	1. Squat
99	2. Leg Press (single leg)
116	3. Power Clean
98	4. Partial Squat
107	5. Stiff-Legged Deadlift
103	6. Sit-up
140	7. Reverse Trunk Twist
122	8. Toe Raise, Leg Press Machine
128	9. Leg Curl
108	10. Bench Press (close grip)
127	11. Cable Pulley Leg Pull
143	12. Frog Hop

Adults and Late Adolescents

Off-Season Program: Two or three training days per week per exercise. Follow the set/rep patterns outlined in the periodization schedule on page 79.

In-Season Program: Two sets of six repetitions at 80 percent of 1RM, two or three training days per week, per exercise.

JUMPER'S PROGRAM

Page	Exercises
99	1. Leg Press (single leg)
101	2. Step-up
115	3. Seated Cable Long Pull
100	4. Lunge
106	5. Stiff-Legged Deadlift
103	6. Sit-up
140	7. Reverse Trunk Twist
122	8. Toe Raise, Leg Press Machine
128	9. Leg Curl
108	10. Bench Press (close grip)
127	11. Cable Pulley Leg Pull
143	12. Frog Hop

Kids and Early Adolescents

First-Year Program: Perform two sets of ten repetitions at 65 percent of 1RM, two days per week throughout the year.

Second-Year Program: Begin a modified off-season periodization schedule as outlined on page 79 after completing the first year of a strength-training program.

POLE VAULT

"Total body movements such as power cleans, Olympic cleans, snatches, or hang cleans are all vital in pole vaulting. Besides strengthening total body parts, less time can be spent in the weight room.

"Possibly the only isolated strength movements needed are knee flexors (hamstring curls), hip flexors (knee raises), and some basic torso work. There is actually no need to isolate other muscles in strength-training sessions unless for rehabilitation."

—Dick Railsback, UCS Incorporated, Lincoln, Nebraska

VAULTER'S PROGRAM

Page	Exercises
98	1. Squat
99	2. Leg Press (single leg)
116	3. Power Clean
140	4. Reverse Trunk Twist
128	5. Leg Curl
127	6. Cable Pulley Leg Pull
111	7. Push Press
105	8. Back Extensions
112	9. Pull-up
130	10. Wrist Curl

Adults and Late Adolexcents

Off-Season Program: Two or three training days per week per exercise. Follow the set/rep patterns outlined in the periodization schedule on page 79.

In-Season Program: Two sets of six repetitions at 80 percent of 1RM, two or three training days per week per exercise.

VAULTER'S PROGRAM

Page	Exercises
99	1. Leg Press (single leg)
101	2. Step-up
115	3. Seated Cable Long Pull
140	4. Reverse Trunk Twist
128	5. Leg Curl
127	6. Cable Pulley Leg Pull
108	7. Bench Press
105	8. Back Extensions
112	9. Pull-up
130	10. Wrist Curl

Kids and Early Adolescents

First-Year Program: Perform two sets of ten repetitions at 65 percent of 1RM, two days per week throughout the year.

Second-Year Program: Begin a modified off-season periodization schedule as outlined on page 79 after completing the first year of a strength-training program.

SPRINTS AND HURDLES

Lee J. Morrow, strength and conditioning coach at East Tennessee State University, suggests that single-leg exercises are important to any speed development program.

Coach Morrow has his athletes perform both double and single-leg exercises. The single-leg exercises, step-ups, and lunges ensure that each leg receives balanced development; too often the athlete favors one leg when performing a two-legged lift such as the squat or leg press. Coach Morrow recommends the following program for his athletes:

Exercises	Sets	Reps
1. Squats*	4	5–8
2. Step-up	3	5–8
3. Lunges	3	5–8
4. Leg Extensions	3	5–8
5. Leg Curl	3	5–8
6. Hip/Back Machine	3	5–8
7. Calf Raises	3	10

* Prepubescents and early adolescents should replace the squat with the leg press, and perform all exercises for two sets of ten reps.

Specificity applied Cable Pulley Leg Pull-up

Stand atop a box and duplicate the knee-lift action of the sprinting motion. Add it to your workout once or twice a week.

Special note on plyometrics

Coaches have become increasingly aware of the eccentric muscle contractions occurring each time the sprinter's foot hits the ground. Plyometrics, a resistance exercise having an eccentric component, are increasingly used as a training tool.

A word of caution: Eccentric contractions tend to induce more-severe, longer-lasting muscular soreness. That makes intense plyometric training a problem for the sprinter during the competitive season. Use plyometrics off-season. The bounding and depth-jump plyometric exercises have been included in the program with the aforementioned cautions.

Special note on injury prevention

Coaches and athletes must design resistance-training programs that balance strength development in opposing muscle groups. Coach Morrow's program points out the correct way. For example, his suggested program includes exercises that develop the quadriceps (squats) and the hamstrings (leg curl)—two opposing muscle groups. Incidentally, the lunges and step-ups work both areas.

SPRINTS PROGRAM
Adults and Late Adolescents

Page	Exercises	Primary Purpose
98	1. Squats	Hip and leg thrust
100	2. Lunges	Hip and leg thrust
104	3. Leg Raises	Knee lift/torso stabilization
140	4. Reverse Trunk Twist	Rotational strength
128	5. Leg Curl	Prevent hamstring injury
110	6. Dip	Arm drive
116	7. Power Clean	Upper-body pull/arm drive
127	8. Low-Pulley	Knee lift/leg pull

Off-Season Program: Two training days per week per exercise following the periodization schedule outlined on page 79.

In-Season Program: Two sets of ten repetitions per set at 70 percent of 1RM; two days per week.

SPRINTS PROGRAM
Kids and Early Adolescents

Page	Exercises	Primary Purpose
100	1. Lunges	Hip and leg thrust
101	2. Step-ups*	Hip and leg thrust
104	3. Leg Raises	Knee lift/torso stabilization
140	4. Reverse Trunk Twist	Trunk rotation/stabilization
128	5. Leg Curl	Prevent injury
108	6. Bench Press	Arm drive (close grip)
112	7. Pull-ups	Upper-body pull
127	8. Low-Pulley Leg Pull	Knee lift
143	9. Frog Hops	Hip and leg drive

* Alternate exercises: Perform leg raises and step-ups during one workout, low-pulley leg pulls and frog hops the next.

Year-round Program: Two sets of ten repetitions per set at 65 percent of 1RM; two training days per week. After a year of steady training, younger athletes can begin a modified off-season periodization schedule as outlined on page 79.

DISTANCE EVENTS

"In the practical world we often encounter situations in which improved strength doesn't bring about the expected speed increases in the athlete's primary event; strength increases sometimes even have a negative effect on competitive results.

"This phenomenon is explained by the fact that many important aspects of sports technique deteriorate during the athlete's transition to intense strength work. The deterioration of these important aspects weakens the athlete's ability to exploit his strength potentials fully.

"These factors should be taken into account in a runner's strength training, and strength training should be combined with technique training. Strength-training exercises should be performed so that they don't disturb, or disrupt, the coordination structure that is inherent in the competitive event."

—V. Kulakov, track coach

The athlete's success in cross-country or the longer track races depends much more on aerobic capacity than muscular strength. But strength training does have its place.

First, strength training reduces the risk of injury, and statistics indicate that the average runner suffers at least one serious injury a year. A strength-trained ankle is less likely to sprain. A stronger knee is less likely to be damaged by leaping into a water pit. A stronger wrist, elbow, and shoulder can better absorb the shock of a fall.

But research has begun to substantiate a more important reason to strength-train: it can inhibit the catabolic response encountered by a runner whose body must scavenge noninvolved tissue to satisfy the demands of too much running.

What type of strength-training workout makes sense for the distance runner? The best bet is a Sports Strength Program supplemented with leg curls, hip flexors, and toe raises. This should take less than one hour, twice each week.

DISTANCE RACE PROGRAM
All Ages

Page	Exercises	Primary Purpose
100	1. Lunge	Hip and leg thrust
101	2. Step-up	Hip and leg thrust
128	3. Leg Curl	Prevent hamstring injuries
107	4. Stiff-Legged Deadlift	Torso stability
108	5. Bench Press (close grip)	Arm drive
112	6. Pull-up	Upper-body pull
122	7. Toe Raise, Leg Press Machine	Ankle extension
127	8. Low-pulley Leg Pull	Knee lift
104	9. Leg Raise	Knee lift/torso stabilization

Year-round Program: Two sets of ten repetitions per set at 65 percent of 1RM; two training days per week.
Note: Strength training helps prevent overall muscle loss due to a distance-training program's catabolic effect.

TRIATHLON

Swimmers swim, cyclists cycle, and runners run, but designing a strength-training program reflecting the triathlon's combined demands is a difficult task.

Triathletes spend most of their training time swimming, running, and cycling; usually two days per week are devoted to each event, leaving little time or energy for a strength program. In fact, the triathlete's potential for overtraining is so great that the Sports Strength Program must be minimized. The dry-land swim machine has been substituted for the upper-body pull and thrust movements of the Sports Strength Program. A torso-strengthening rotational movement has been added to counterbalance the lower-back stress encountered during triathlon training and competition.

TRIATHLON PROGRAM
All Ages

Page	Exercises	Primary Purpose
100	1. Lunge	Leg and hip thrust
140	2. Reverse Trunk Twist	Rotational strength: torso stabilization
193	3. Swim Machine	Event-specific
107	4. Stiff-Legged Deadlift	Back extension/protection
132	5. Alternating Upright Row	Balance shoulder development

Year-round Program: Adults and late adolescents train two or three days per week, three sets of ten reps at 60 percent of 1RM. Kids and early adolescents train twice per week, two sets of ten repetitions at 60 percent of 1RM.

Note on stationary cycling: Keep in mind that a stationary bike is a good way to build muscular and aerobic endurance, but doesn't increase strength.

VOLLEYBALL

"A combination of strength, power, agility, and both aerobic and anaerobic endurance is required in today's volleyball player. Not only must players jump high and move quickly to the ball, they must have endurance to play competitively during games extended over very long periods of time. Considering that a match is three out of five games, it is not unusual to see a match last three hours or longer. It is also common for players to compete in several matches on the same day. For this reason, it is evident that emphasis should be placed on the conditioning program of a collegiate volleyball team."

—Laura Dunnam and Dr. Gary Hunter, University of Alabama at Birmingham, Department of Health, Physical Education and Recreation

Special note on jumping

Numerous studies have validated that strength training improves vertical jumping ability, an important skill during strong play close to the net.

Maximum jump height depends partly on inherited factors, including the ratio of fast- and slow-twitch muscle fibers, and tendon attachments' positions on the bones.

Whatever your inherited potential, you can improve your vertical jump through strength training. You can't exceed your genetic limitations, but until you reach your genetically defined strength limitation—which is unlikely—your jump will improve.

VOLLEYBALL PROGRAM
Adults and Late Adolescents

Page	Exercises	Primary Purpose
98	1. Squat	Hip and leg thrust
101	2. Step-up or lunge	Hip and leg thrust
113	3. Lat Pull-down	Upper-body pull
108	4. Bench Press (incline)	Upper-body thrust
125	5. Bent-Arm DB Pullover	Spike pull-through
121	6. Toe Raise	Ankle extension during jump
104	7. Leg Raise	Knee lift/torso stabilization
107	8. Straight-Leg Deadlift	Back extension during jump
130	9. Wrist Curl	Wrist flexion during hit
155	10. Hand Rings	Ball control

Off-Season Program: Follow the set/rep patterns outlined in the periodization program found in page 79.

In-Season: Two sets of ten repetitions, two training days per week. Each set at 70 percent 1RM.

Plyometrics: Depth jumps and frog hops can be included in the strength-building program. Directions for these exercises are found on page 143.

VOLLEYBALL PROGRAM
Adults and Late Adolescents

Page	Exercises	Primary Purpose
99	1. Leg Press	Hip and leg thrust
100	2. Lunge	Hip and leg thrust
114	3. Bent-Over Row	Upper-body pull
125	4. Bent-Arm DB Pullover	Spike Pull-through
121	5. Toe Raise	Ankle-extension strength during jump
104	6. Leg Raise	Knee lift
105	7. Back Extension	Back extension during jump
130	8. Wrist Curl	Wrist flexion during hit
155	9. Hand Rings	Ball control

Year-round Program: After a year of steady training, kids and early adolescents can begin a modified periodization training program that is individually prescribed by a professional. Until that time, younger athletes should train twice each week throughout the year: two sets of ten repetitions, at 65 percent of 1RM.

WRESTLING

"It has been said that strength is what makes technique work. It is obvious to most people in wrestling that one without the other is of little use. Strength training can also be employed in wrestling to enhance muscular endurance and to prevent and rehabilitate injuries.

"Many people believe that if you lift weights and gain strength you will also gain weight. Although this can be the case, it does not have to be. A wrestler following a proper diet (basically high carbohydrate, moderate protein, and low fat) and using a three-times-per-week lifting routine emphasizing high reps (ten to twelve) and a moderate number of sets (three to five) per muscle group can experience significant gains in strength and power over a period of time without a correspondingly significant increase in weight.

"A second misconception is that wrestling practice and competition alone will maintain strength and power in season. This, too, is incorrect based on our experience that 'hard' wrestling and running without routine maintenance lifting will often result in loss of muscle mass."

—Mark Johnson, Head wrestling coach, Oregon State University, and Charles Yesalis, Ph.D.

All other factors being equal, a stronger wrestler is a better wrestler. But *all* factors are never equal. Each wrestler is a unique package of skills, motivation, quickness, endurance, and strength. Consequently, each wrestler's training program should emphasize the factors that will improve his overall performance.

The path begins with a balanced analysis of the athlete's long-term goals. A very thin wrestler may hope to move up several classes, adding muscular body weight and strength. Another wrestler might want to increase strength without adding bulk. Yet another might focus on improved endurance. Once realistic goals are determined, the coach and wrestler can chart an appropriate training program.

All members of a wrestling team share common denominators. Strength training is one. At the collegiate level, off-season heavy-lifting programs are prescribed from April through August, in-season programs continue September through January, and postseason low-intensity circuit programs allow recovery during February and March.

High school schedules differ, usually running November through February. The lifting schedule is accordingly shuffled as the following chart indicates.

POST
SEASON
Light
Conditioning
MARCH &
APRIL

IN SEASON
2-3 days/week
2 sets/6 reps
NOV. through
FEB.

OFF SEASON
Heavy lifting
MAY through OCT.

Strength vs. Endurance

The wrestler's relative dependence on strength or endurance fluctuates throughout a match. Jim Klinzing, Ph.D., puts it best in the *National Strength and Conditioning Association Journal*: "During the initial stages of a match, strength and power are the primary factors needed to achieve a pin or to avoid being pinned. . . . A wrestler must reach that second or third period to take advantage of muscular endurance."

Injury Prevention

Inadequate strength is the cause of the most common wrestling injury—a strained neck—particularly in middle and high school.

Often the athlete uses the head as a contact point for a back bridge while trying to avoid a pin. The combined weight of the athlete and his opponent exceed the young wrestler's muscular capacity. Try the following movements to condition the neck before initiating contact training.

WRESTLING PROGRAM

Page	Exercises
116	1. Power Clean
115	2. Cable Pulley Long Pull
108	3. Bench Press
114	4. Bent-Over Dumbbell Row
98	5. Squats
99	6. Leg Press
111	7. Push Press
136	8. Dumbbell Biceps Curl
128	9. Leg Curl
118	10. Barbell High Pull
107	11. Stiff-Legged Deadlift
140	12. Reverse Trunk Twist
103	13. Sit-up

Adults/Late Adolescents

Off-Season: Two or three training days per week per exercise. Follow the set/rep patterns outlined in the periodization schedule on page 79.

In-Season: Two sets of six repetitions at 80 percent of 1RM, two or three training days per week per exercise.

WRESTLING PROGRAM

Page	Exercises
115	1. Cable Pulley Long Pull
112	2. Pull-up
108	3. Bench Press
114	4. Bent-Over Dumbbell Row
102	5. Hack Squat*
99	6. Leg Press
132	7. Alternate Upright Row
136	8. Dumbbell Biceps Curl
128	9. Leg Curl
105	10. Back Extension
140	11. Reverse Trunk Twist
103	12. Sit-up

Kids/Early Adolescents

First-Year Program: Perform two sets of ten repetitions at 65 percent of 1RM, two days per week throughout the year.

Second-Year Program: Begin a modified off-season periodization schedule as outlined on page 79 after completing the first year of a strength-training program.

BIBLIOGRAPHY AND SOURCES

GENERAL REFERENCES

Abel, Bob, and Valenti, Michael. *Sports Quotes: The Insider's View of the Sports World*. New York: Facts on File, 1983.

Berger, Richard A. *Introduction to Weight Training*. Englewood Cliffs, NJ: Prentice-Hall, 1984.

Brooks, George A., and Fahey, Thomas D. *Fundamentals of Human Performance*. New York: Macmillan, 1987.

Bursztyn, Peter G. *Physiology for Sportspeople: A Serious User's Guide to the Body*. New York: Manchester University Press, 1990.

Butts, Nancy K.; Gushiken, Thomas T.; and Zarins, Bertram. *The Elite Athlete*. New York: Spectrum, 1985.

Cureton, Thomas K., Jr., ed. *Encyclopedia of Physical Education, Fitness, and Sports. Volume Four: Human Performance: Efficiency and Improvements in Sports, Exercise, and Fitness*. Reston, VA: American Alliance for Health, Physical Education, Recreation, and Dance (AAHPERD), 1985.

Fleck, Steven J., and Kraemer, William J. *Designing Resistance Training Programs*. Champaign, IL: Human Kinetics, 1987.

Green, Lee, ed. *Sportswit*. New York: Harper & Row, 1984.

Jensen, Clayne R., and Fisher, A. G. *Scientific Basis of Athletic Conditioning*. Philadelphia: Lea & Febiger, 1979.

Johnson, Arthur T. *Biomechanics and Exercise Physiology*. New York: John Wiley & Sons, 1991.

Johnston, Francis E., ed. *Nutritional Anthropology*. New York: Alan R. Liss, 1987.

Kirby, Ronald, and Roberts, John A. *Introductory Biomechanics*. Ithaca, NY: Mouvement, 1985.

Lathrop, Jim, and Stoessel, Lynne. "The Bunt." *National Strength and Conditioning Association Journal* 13.3 (1991): 6–8.

McDonagh, M. J. N., and Davies, C. T. M. "Adaptive Response of Mammalian Skeletal Muscle to Exercise with High Loads." *European Journal of Applied Physiology* 52 (1984): 139.

Micheli, Lyle J., ed. *Pediatric and Adolescent Sports Medicine.* Boston: Little, Brown, 1984.

Oseid, Svein, and Carlsen, Kai-Håkon, eds. *Children and Exercise XIIIth International Congress on Pediatric Work Physiology.* Champaign, IL: Human Kinetics, 1989.

Poprawski, Bogdan C. "Aspects of Strength, Power, and Speed in Shot Put Training." *National Strength and Conditioning Association Journal,* 9.6 (1987): 39–41.

Sharkey, Brian J. *Coaches Guide to Sport Physiology.* Champaign, IL: Human Kinetics, 1986.

Stearn, William. "Weight Training for Men's Gymnastics." *National Strength and Conditioning Association Journal* 8.5 (1986): 50–51.

Totten, Leo. "General Safety Considerations for the Power Clean." *National Strength and Conditioning Association Journal* 8.5 (1986): 65–67.

Voy, Robert, with Deeter, Kirk D. *Drugs, Sport, and Politics.* Champaign, IL: Human Kinetics, 1991.

Wright, James E., and Cowart, Virginia S. *Anabolic Steroids: Altered States.* Carmel, IN: Benchmark, 1990.

INDIVIDUAL SPORTS

Archery   Williams, J. C. *Archery for Beginners.* Chicago: Contemporary Books. 1985.

Baseball   Jacobs, P. "The Overhand Baseball Pitch: A Kinesiological Analysis and Related Strength-Conditioning Programming." *National Strength and Conditioning Association Journal* 9.1 (1987): 5–13.

Roll, F.; Omer, J.; and Pontiff, W. "Tulane Off-season Baseball Program." *National Strength and Conditioning Association Journal* 8.2 (1986): 38–41.

Basketball   Chandler, J. "Goals and Activities for Athletic Conditioning in Basketball." *National Strength and Conditioning Association Journal* 8.5 (1986): 52–55.

Bicycling   Klausen, K. *Physiology of Sport,* ed. T. Reilly et al. London: E. & F. Spon. 1990.

Bowling   DeBenedette, V. "Exercise That'll Bowl You Over." *The Physician and Sportsmedicine* 19.3 (1991): 180–184.

Boxing   Dengel, D. R., George, T. W., Bainbridge, C., et al. "Training Responses in National Team Boxers." *Medical Science Sports Exercise,* 1987; 19 (April suppl): S47.

Lundberg, G. D., and Litel, G. R. "A Round Table: The Medical Aspects of Boxing." *The Physician and Sportsmedicine* 13.9 (1985): 58–72.

Fencing Dempsey, Y. "A Conditioning Program for Women Fencers." *Selected Fencing Articles*, ed. M. Herndon. Washington, DC: American Association for Health, Physical Education, and Recreation, 1971.

Football Miller, A. "Karl Mecklenburg, Denver Broncos Interview." *National Strength and Conditioning Association Journal* 11.3 (1989): 74–75.

Ohton, D. "A Kinesiological Look at the Long Snap in Football." *National Strength and Conditioning Association Journal* 10.1 (1988): 4–13.

Golf Wren, G. "Nautilus and Golf: The Do's and Don'ts." *Golf Digest* 37.1 (1986): 77–79.

Martial Arts Hemba, G. "A Contemporary Application to Sports Strength and Conditioning." *National Strength and Conditioning Association Journal* 13.2 (1991): 31–34.

McGuire, M. "Get the Angle on Training." *Martial Arts Training* 8.1 (1991): 62–63.

Wong, S. "Can't Have One Without the Other: The Balance between Strength and Skill." *Martial Arts Training* 18.2 (1991): 64–65.

Rowing Lezotte, S. *Sportsperformance: Rowing Power and Endurance.* Chicago: Contemporary Books, 1987, page 1.

Skiing O'Shea, P. "Nordic Skiing—the Diagonal Stride and Ski Skating." *National Strength and Conditioning Association Journal* 9.6 (1987): 4–12.

Tennis Groppel, J. L.; Conroy, B.; and Hubb, E. "The Mechanics of the Tennis Forehand Drive: Suggestions for Training the Tennis Player." *National Strength and Conditioning Association Journal* 8.5 (1986): 5–10.

Track and Field: THROWS Erickson, M. "The Big 3 Exercises in Shot-put Training." *Scholastic Coach* April 1989: 16–17.

Lukens, D. "Rotation Shot Put for Beginners." *Track and Field Quarterly Review* 83.3 (1989): 9.

O'Shea, P. "Throwing Speed: Throwing Demands Upper Body Power." *Track and Field Quarterly Review* 31.3 (1991): 39.

HIGH JUMP Reid, P. "Approach and Take-Off for the Back Lay-Out High Jump." *National Strength and Conditioning Association Journal* 8.1 (1986): 5–7.

POLE VAULT Railsback, D. "The Pole Vault." *National Strength and Conditioning Association Journal* 9.2 (1987): 6–8.

SPRINTS AND HURDLES Morrow, L. J. "Single Leg Strength: Its Relationship to Speed Enhancement." *National Strength and Conditioning Association Journal* 18.5 (1986): 64–65.

DISTANCE RUNNING Kulakov, V. "The Harmony of Training: The Training of Long-Distance Runners." *Soviet Sports Review* 24.4 (1989): 165–168.

Volleyball Dunnam, L. O.; Hunter, G. R.; Williams, B. P.; and Dremsa, C. J. "University of Alabama at Birmingham Women's Volleyball Year-Round Training Program." *National Strength and Conditioning Association Journal* 10.1 (1988): 50–52.

Wrestling Camaione, D., and Klinzing, J. "Strength Training and Conditioning for Wrestling, Part II." *National Strength and Conditioning Association Journal* 8.3 (1988): 12–23.

Johnson, M., and Yesalis, C. "Strength Training and Conditioning for Wrestling: The Iowa Approach." *National Strength and Conditioning Association Journal* 8.4 (1986): 56–59.

SPECIALIZED PERFORMANCE

Hand Strength "For Grip Strength and Range of Motion" (booklet). Oakbrook, IL: Exerquipment, 1990: 1–10.

Jumping Cureton, T. K. Jr., "Mechanics and Kinesiology of the High Jump." *Encyclopedia of Physical Education, Fitness, and Sports*, vol. 4. *Human Performance: Efficiency and Improvements in Sports, Exercise, and Fitness*, ed. T. K. Cureton, Jr. Reston, VA: AAHPERD, 1985: 537–541.

Kirby, R., and Roberts, J. A. *Introductory Biomechanics*. Ithaca, NY: Mouvement, 1985.

Klinzing, J. E. "Training for Improved Jumping Ability of Basketball Players." *National Strength and Conditioning Association Journal* 10.3 (1988): 61–64.

Speed Korchemny, R. "Training with the Objective to Improve Stride Length." *National Strength and Conditioning Association Journal* 13.3 (1991): 27–32.

McFarlane, B. "A Look Inside the Biomechanics and Dynamics of Speed." *National Strength and Conditioning Association Journal* 9.5 (1987): 35–41.

Morrow, L. J. "Single Leg Strength: Its Relationship to Speed Enhancement." *National Strength and Conditioning Association Journal* 18.5 (1986): 64–65.

Swing Groppel, J. L., and Conroy, B. "The Mechanics of the Tennis Forehand Drive: Suggestions for Training the Tennis Player." *National Strength and Conditioning Association Journal* 8.5 (1986): 5–10.

SIDEBAR SOURCES

Page

16   *Los Angeles Times*, December 23,1991: C2.
48   *Los Angeles Times*, August TK, 1991, sports section, Box.
52   Udell Dean, M.D. national syndicated radio show, January 16, 1992.
53   *Los Angeles Times*, December 29, 1991: C2.
56   Elia, Irene. *The Female Animal*. New York: Henry Holt, 1988.
57   Lyle Alzado interview with Larry King, CNN, January 4, 1991.
60   *Physician's Desk Reference*, 1970.
145   Smith, Shelley. "Heavy Duty." *Sports Illustrated* 75.3 (July 15, 1991): 43.
183   Hemba, Gary. "A Contemporary Application to Sports Strength and Conditioning." *National Strength and Conditioning Association Journal* 13.2 (1991): 31–41.

EXERCISE EQUIPMENT DIRECTORY

Cybex Equipment
2100 Smithtown Avenue
P.O. Box 9003
Ronkonkoma, NY 11779-0903

Exerquipment, Inc. (Exer-Rings)
616 Enterprise Drive
Oakbrook, IL 60521

Fitness Trend/Fitness Systems (Swim Machine)
P.O. Box 266
Independence, MO 64051

Flex Equipment
1525 W. Orange Grove Street
Orange, CA 92068

Hydra Fitness
P.O. Box 599
Belton, Texas 76513

Power-stik™
3342 Rose Lane
Falls Church, VA 22042

Soloflex, Inc.
Hawthorne Farm Industrial Park
Hillsboro, Oregon 97124-6494

Universal Gym Equipment, Inc.
930 27th Avenue, S.W.
Box 1270
Cedar Rapids, Iowa 52406

Vasa Swim Trainer
372 Governor Chittenden Road
Williston, Vermont 95495

MODELS IN SPORTS STRENGTH

Bruce Budzik:
Bruce combines graduate school in biology with competitive body-building.

Nathan Funnell:
Nathan competed in high school track, concentrating on the shot put and discus.

Owen Engelmann:
A former collegiate wrestler, Owen is an educational consultant who weight-trains and competes in handball tournaments.

Robert Hausmann:
An all-around athlete, Robert used weight training to compete successfully at the collegiate level in football and track.

Heather Fitzgerald:
Heather combines high school with a part-time job, aerobics, and competition in track and soccer.

Emilio Hernandez, Jr.:
Having started weight training with high school wrestling and football, Emilio continues to lift for bodybuilding and conditioning while effectively balancing the demands of university administration and family.

Andrew Hunt:
A high school student, Andrew was national Junior Olympic 3,000 meters champion as a sixteen-year-old.

Lori Sonneburg:
A hospital administrator, Lori dedicates her free time to weight training and bodybuilding.

John Lassen:
John used weight training to build a successful high school football career and continues to train as a hobby.

Chris Sprague:
A weight lifter since he was nine years old, Chris is a four-time national champion in the shot and discus—and he's only thirteen.

Sandy Newton:
A certified physical education and aerobics teacher, Sandy finished seventh in the 800-meter run in the 1989 World Veterans Games.

Jennifer Waldrop:
An athlete and aspiring model, Jennifer competes in high school track and volleyball.

Ember Parks:
An all-around athlete, Ember competes in high school track and swimming.

Kendra Yamamoto:
Kendra currently competes in high school volleyball and softball, and enjoys swimming.

Larry Smith:
A university administrator, Larry both competes in and organizes cycling events in the Northwest, and plays racquetball.

ABOUT THE AUTHOR

Ken Sprague has personally trained and coached athletes of all ages, at all competitive levels, both amateurs and professionals, beginners and world champions. He owned and operated the original Gold's Gym for a decade, and is author of *The Gold's Gym Weight Training Book*, *The Gold's Gym Strength Training Book*, *The Athlete's Body*, and *Weight and Strength Training for Kids and Teenagers*. Ken's thirty-five years of practical weight-training experience are supported by a Phi Beta Kappa science degree and advanced training in sports physiology and psychology. He teaches high school chemistry and biology, and lives with his family in Eugene, Oregon.

Ken's younger son, Chris, is a thirteen-year-old weight trainer and has won three Junior Olympic National Championships in the shot put and discus throw. His older son, Ken Jr., played college basketball.